Child of the Apocalypse

Child of the Apocalypse

Ellen G. White

DONALD EDWARD CASEBOLT

WIPF & STOCK · Eugene, Oregon

CHILD OF THE APOCALYPSE
Ellen G. White

Copyright © 2021 Donald Edward Casebolt. All rights reserved. Except for brief quotations in critical publications or reviews, no part of this book may be reproduced in any manner without prior written permission from the publisher. Write: Permissions, Wipf and Stock Publishers, 199 W. 8th Ave., Suite 3, Eugene, OR 97401.

Wipf & Stock
An Imprint of Wipf and Stock Publishers
199 W. 8th Ave., Suite 3
Eugene, OR 97401

www.wipfandstock.com

PAPERBACK ISBN: 978-1-6667-1961-1
HARDCOVER ISBN: 978-1-6667-1962-8
EBOOK ISBN: 978-1-6667-1963-5

OCTOBER 20, 2021

"We are all tattooed in our cradles with the beliefs of our tribe; the record may seem superficial, but it is indelible."

OLIVER WENDELL HOLMES

Contents

Preface	ix
Acknowledgments	xix
Introduction: *Child* of the Apocalypse, Ellen Harmon White	1
Aurora Borealis of February 1837, Meteorite Shower of 1833, Dark Day of 1780	9
Capacity of Debilitated Twelve-Year-Old to Evaluate Miller's Fifteen Proofs	14
Twelve-Year-Old Ellen Harmon's Lack of the Assurance of Salvation	18
Primordial Proofs: 1) "Many Proofs" and "Startling Facts" 2) "Tornado" of the Holy Spirit	20
Buxton Camp Meeting's Ecstatic Experience for Thirteen-Year-Old Ellen	21
Elder Stockman and Fourteen-Year-Old Ellen	24
Fifteen-Year-Old Ellen's Assurance of Salvation Came Via the Message of "Definite Time"	26
Foy's "Rolling Mountains of Flame" Paralleled Miller's Message of Hell, Hell, Hell	27

Mere Days before March 21, 1844 Ellen Exposed to Foy's Ecstatic Hellfire Preaching	29
Ezekiel 12, Habakkuk 2, and Jeremiah 51: Snow's Proofs of a Tarrying Time and Midnight Cry	30
Fifteen-Year-Old Ellen Initiates Her Career as Public Visionary, Evangelist, and Speaker	33
Imprinting, "Train Up a Child," "As the Twig Is Bent the Tree Is Inclined"	39
Mental Capacity	42
Caleb Rich, Universalist Visionary	52
Richard Randel, Freewill Baptist Founder	54
Father Pearson and Portland Church Ratify Ellen's Divine Call	56
Ellen's Sleigh Ride to Avoid J. Turner's Bridegroom Doctrine	59
Ellen Harmon's First Vision Confirms Snow's Midnight Cry	60
Nichols's 1851 Chart Replaces Miller's 1843 Chart per White's Authority	62
Miller's Erroneous Theories vs. Common Sense Truths	64
Bernadette Soubirous and Lourdes: Psycho-Social Milieu Like EGW's	68
Joan of Arc's Similarities with Ellen Harmon	73
Conclusion	83
Bibliography	95

Preface

"We are all tattooed in our cradles with the beliefs of our tribe; the record may seem superficial, but it is indelible."
OLIVER WENDELL HOLMES

MY SPIRITUAL CRADLE WAS a Seventh-day Adventist (SDA) church. Both my maternal and paternal grandparents were Seventh-day Adventists. Several of my earliest memories involve singing Sabbath school songs and memorizing Bible texts. When the Roseburg SDA church built a new sanctuary in about 1962 when I was twelve, my mother was proud that her son was the first male baptized in its baptismal fount. I attended Seventh-day Adventist parochial schools at an elementary level, secondary level, and university level, graduating from Andrews University in 1972. I was admitted to the Masters of Divinity program at Andrews University where I studied from the fall of 1974 through the summer of 1976. I then studied Hebrew and Theology at the University of Tübingen in Germany one academic year. The following two years I was in a doctoral program in Northwest Semitic languages (including the biblical languages of Hebrew and Aramaic) at the University of Chicago. At Andrews I became aware of Ellen G. White's extensive borrowings from Protestant historians. I determined to study this independently for myself and chose to compare Ellen G. White's description of the Waldenses with one of her Protestant

Preface

sources, Wylie. I documented in two parallel columns a pattern of Ellen G. White's literary dependence on Wylie. These consisted of both loose and tight paraphrases. I then published a manuscript demonstrating this in the February 1981 edition of *Spectrum*. I entitled it: "Ellen White, the Waldenses, and Historical Interpretation." In polemical debates between the Catholics and Protestants, Catholics asserted that their heritage and legitimacy was based on apostolic succession and Christ's promise to his disciples that the gates of hell would never prevail against this church. They accused Protestants of being upstart parvenus. In response, Protestants regularly identified the Waldenses as being pure descendants of apostolic Christianity and traced their spiritual roots to them. However, Protestants, including the Millerites, never asserted that the Waldenses were Sabbath-keepers. Ellen G. White made the novel claim that they had hallowed Sabbath since apostolic times. I discovered that this is simply factually untrue. I also became aware that several other concepts that she asserted that she was shown in vision were factually incorrect, such as her assertion that masturbation caused an epidemic of insanity and a whole host of other loathsome diseases. Defenses made by denominationally employed apologists presumed that whatever Ellen G. White stated she was shown in vision were direct emanations of the divine Mind. They therefore insisted that everything she said, although not formally inerrant, was substantially correct with the possible exception of a few apparent inconsistencies in matters of little consequence.

On the opposite pole, persons like Walter T. Rea in *The White Lie* implied she was a conscious fraud. My independent conclusion was that Ellen G. White did not intend to deceive. Rather, she was factually mistaken regarding matters of more than "little consequence" without being aware that she was factually mistaken. It would certainly not be the first case in which a religious leader was completely mistaken about a very sincerely held belief. In any case, I determined that since I could not support the "orthodox" denominational explanation for Ellen G. White's borrowed and inaccurate statements, I should drop my career plan of teaching Hebrew at an SDA university and terminate my doctoral studies. I switched

Preface

careers, eventually becoming a Family Nurse Practitioner. However, for about three decades several files regarding these issues lay dormant in file boxes. Upon retirement I resumed my examination of extrabiblical sources that Ellen G. White used. In the interim, more scholarly literature had accumulated and more was available electronically on the internet. I was surprised to learn that in her First Vision she paraphrased material from the pseudepigraphal book of 2 Esdras to describe what she "saw" in her tour in heaven, even behind the second veil to the Most Holy Place. In short, she was dependent upon noncanonical sources from her earliest writings. This was not a late development as she expanded her initial 1860s version of the *Great Controversy* to an 1880s multi-volume series relying extensively on Protestant historians. Furthermore, it seemed clear that she had *unconsciously* copied 2 Esdras and other apocryphal sources as if they were protocanonical because 2 Esdras was in her very own 1822 family King James Version. Further research demonstrated that, by far, William Miller was her most bountiful source. He was an immense influence on Ellen Harmon. As the Father Miller of Millerism, it was only to be expected that he would have had an outsized influence on Ellen Harmon. However, no one had previously explicitly described, case-by-case, the collection of Millerite prophetic interpretations that Ellen not only inherited from Miller but were demonstrably farfetched, fanciful, and just plain erroneous, even according to the dean of SDA apologists who wrote *The Midnight Cry*. This was the proverbial elephant hidden in the room. Obviously, Ellen Harmon was a *child* of the Apocalypse and she was Father Miller's spiritual daughter. But no one had previously pointed out that besides being mistaken in predicting the Second Coming for October 22, 1844, Miller had made a whole host of other erroneous assertions that Ellen Harmon had copied. Miller's erroneous methodology and results were inconsistent with Ellen Harmon's assertion that God guided him in his interpretation of Daniel and Revelation. Furthermore, no one had ever noted that Miller, who claimed to merely let the Bible interpret itself with only the help of a concordance, actually was enormously dependent upon the hoary tradition of the allegorical-typological-historicist method. Ellen Harmon believed Miller's self-conception and even reinforced it, believing that she had seen God sending Miller regular angelic guidance in interpreting the prophecies of Daniel and Revelation.

Concurrently, I realized that Ellen Harmon was a mere prepubescent of twelve when she personally encountered Miller and his fifteen proofs that predicted the Second Coming in 1843–44. Furthermore, she was mentally incapacitated at the time. Her severe brain trauma had forced her to drop out of a female seminary just months before her encounter with Miller because she was *mentally incapable of absorbing her school work*. SDA apologists themselves stated that her central nervous system was "shattered."[1] Ellen herself stated that had she continued her schooling, it would have killed her.[2]

In addition to her mental immaturity and damaged brain during her critical encounter with Father Miller at age twelve, William Foy's out-of-body experiences were also formative and normative for Ellen Harmon. Most SDAs are vaguely aware that Ellen Harmon inherited her prophetic mantel from William Foy. They are not aware that he claimed to have out-of-body visions lasting up to twelve hours during which a physician certified that he was not breathing and had only a little activity around his heart. They are not aware that his visions were proclaimed in support of Miller's setting a definite time in 1843–44 for the Second Coming. They are not aware that only about a week prior to March 21, 1844 (the date Miller initially set for the Second Coming) Ellen Harmon attended a lecture series by William Foy in which he asserted that those who did not accept Miller's message would be burnt alive in the cleansing fire of the Second Coming. In short, young Ellen Harmon, with a shattered central nervous system, was confronted with a whole concatenation of forces which bound her inextricably to Miller's message. She states that she was saved through Miller's date-setting message and that this was ratified by ecstatic, out-of-body experiences and divinely inspired dreams that proved that

---

1. Coon, *Great Visions of Ellen G. White*, 172.
2. White, *Life Sketches*, 26.

Preface

God was "in" the proclamation of October 22, 1844 for the Second Coming. As the Bible itself says: "Train up a child in the way he should go, and when he is old, he will not depart from it."[3]

Ellen Harmon White, the *child* of the Apocalypse, Father Miller's daughter, was tattooed by Miller's message and *method*. And due to her untiring efforts, both Miller's message and method have been tattooed into the DNA of SDA theology. For example, despite the fact that the Ottoman Empire never collapsed on August 11, 1840, as predicted by the Millerites, Ellen G. White asserts that it did. About twenty similarly erroneous eschatological interpretations still saturate SDA theology. These originated in pre-Miller sources. Miller inherited them, Ellen Harmon inherited them from Miller, and SDA thought leaders inherited them from Ellen Harmon-White. Currently, the SDA church feels constrained to support such interpretations because Ellen G. White asserted that her visions confirmed that such erroneous interpretations were divinely endorsed. It's tattooed indelibly.

There are numerous references to the fact that Ellen G. White had a virtual obsession with her role as Messenger. She tells several anecdotes whose moral is that if she declines God's command to be his Messenger, she will be committing the unpardonable sin. Frequently she and others mention the fact that she wrote, if not compulsively, then almost continually during her waking hours. For example, on July 4, 1859 she tersely noted: "Wrote nearly all day—important matter."[4] Willie White testified that on a typical day his mother had already been writing for three hours by 6:00 a.m. when the rest of the family awoke, and that after breakfast and worship, she "would fill out the morning with a few hours of writing."[5] Regularly, Ellen G. White would awake around 2:00 or 3:00 a.m. and write for hours. This is not surprising given the fact that the Ellen G. White Estates calculated that Ellen G. White had over two thousand visions—far more than all the Old and New Testament writers combined! If one has the self-perception

---

3. Prov 22:6, KJV.
4. White, *Letters and Manuscripts*, 637.
5. Knight, *Walking with Ellen White*, 89–90.

PREFACE

that one has been gifted with over two thousand vitally important visions that will determine the eternal destiny of millions of persons, it is to be expected that that person would make it their highest priority to preach and write compulsively. Thus, Knight states that Ellen G. White wrote over eight thousand letters and five thousand periodical articles in order to communicate her two thousand visions.[6] While William Miller was capable of admitting that his 1843–44 predictions were in no manner fulfillments of prophecy, Ellen Harmon would insist that Millerism was a direct fulfillment of the first two angels of Rev 14, and that God was in the date-setting of both March 21, 1844 and October 22, 1844. Psychologically, she had been imprinted with Miller's results and methods and found it impossible to interpret events of the Millerite movement in any other way. Even after the Father Miller of Millerism had himself repudiated his previous date-setting.

As a result of the facts in primary sources, I became convinced that Ellen Harmon was not consciously prevaricating; she was simply persistently wrong, or to put it more dramatically, deluded. Deluded in an objectively clinical sense, not in a pejorative sense. By deluded I simply mean being persistently mistaken despite overwhelming evidence to the contrary. It is difficult for any of us to conceive of how another person could so emphatically and insistently promulgate a narrative obviously incongruent with reality except that that person is intending to deceive.

However, when one of my loved ones was diagnosed with schizophrenia, I became deeply conscious of the fact that *persons can be totally convinced of the reality of ideas and concepts that have no basis in objective reality*. Schizophrenia, for example, is accompanied about 50 percent of the time by anosognosia. Anosognosia is the condition of having a mental pathology but being totally unaware that one has a mental pathology. In a typical case, a person suffering from schizophrenia may have delusions, auditory or visual, that they are certain are objectively real. Similarly, persons may resort to confabulation. This is a condition in which a person relates a narrative which has no basis in objective reality but which

---

6. Knight, *Walking with Ellen White*, 119.

they are absolutely convinced is true. I believe the phenomenon of anosognosia and confabulation are on a continuous spectrum which includes the psycho-social condition known as cognitive dissonance. This is well known as a phenomenon of socially isolated small groups. At times these small groups make eschatological predictions which are falsified by events. But rather than changing their prophetic schemas, they perseverate in them. They reinterpret events, that for most persons would be considered plain falsifications, as still being consistent with their original predictions.

When do phenomena such as illogical thinking or cognitive dissonance border on physiological pathologies such as anosognosia, confabulation, and delusion? The recent coronavirus pandemic illustrates this fuzzy border. I spoke to both family and friends who perseverated in describing it as a hoax, exaggeration, or "fake news," even when temporary refrigerator morgues are parked outside hospital ICUs because regular morgues were overrun. Even when hundreds of thousands have died in India, Brazil, and the United States. My colleagues, in my opinion, were so emotionally and epistemologically attached to a narrative that minimized the pandemic, that they were deluded. *No amount of empirical evidence could sway their opinion.* Now that in autumn 2021 India and Brazil are being hit with a tsunami wave, are they still convinced that this is fake news? Is their persistent resistance to a concrete, visible, physical reality a pathological, severe mental illness akin to schizophrenia or is it "simply" stubborn wrongheadedness?

Considering Ellen G. White's earliest childhood religious experiences, I believed she exhibited too much sincerity and genuine piety to be a conscious fraud when she was seventeen. She lived in a time and place where the Apocalypse was a lived reality. From about age eight to age fifteen, she lived in a continual torment, fearing that she would inevitably burn eternally in hell. At age nine she had a traumatic brain injury that almost killed her and set the course for her entire life. She begins her several autobiographies with this seminal incident and says it was to impact her entire life, but its ramifications have never been adequately considered. She was still mentally disabled when she first encountered William

Preface

Miller's fifteen mathematical proofs that Christ's Second Coming was divinely programmed for 1843–44. She was overwhelmed by both the math and the textual proof texts. She simply drew the wrong conclusions. Miller's system was a proverbial house of cards. A retrospective examination of his interpretations and methods demonstrates this objectively—beyond a reasonable doubt. Miller's enormous influence on her has never been fully appreciated. She asserted that God regularly sent him angels that guided him to his fifteen proofs. Thus, even when Miller's third date for the end of the world came and went, Ellen G. White was still convinced that God was "in" his and S. S. Snow's prediction that the Second Coming would occur on October 22, 1844. Within a few months after this date, Ellen G. White, Joseph Turner, O. R. L. Crosier, and a few others, developed an alternative "Coming" that allowed them to insist that God had still inspired their original message that the Second Coming was divinely programmed for October 22, 1844. Their revised hypothesis was that Christ had come *invisibly* as High Priest into the heavenly Most Holy on October 22, 1844. Christ would come *visibly* as King within a few months—which stretched into years. Repeatedly, especially during the interval 1845–1851, Ellen G. White insisted that Christ would come within months. As late as May 27, 1856 she insisted that some hearing her voice would be translated without dying. She even puts this assertion into the mouth of her angelic guide in formal quotations: Some of the company present at the Battle Creek conference in 1856 "will be alive and remain upon the earth to be translated at the coming of Jesus."[7] Frequently, she refers to translation as an imminent event.

It was indispensable to her role as Messenger that she had an *absolute conviction* that all the material she perceived in her visions or dreams came as *direct emanations from the divine mind*. Her first disciples formally voted statements to this effect. This indelibly tattooed the nascent movement accreting around Ellen Harmon. Therefore, any empirical information from any source which contradicted this belief was anathema which was impossible for

---

7. White, *Early Years*, 338–39.

her to envision. She was no more aware of confabulation than the schizophrenic with anosognosia is aware that their delusions are not real. The historical analysis of how the *child* of the Apocalypse became the Messenger is recounted from Ellen G. White's own accounts and from contemporary Millerite literature of the 1840s. Because I realize that this is a novel paradigm, perhaps as difficult to conceive of as "continental drift" was in the 1930s, I have concluded my analysis of Ellen Harmon with a few brief sketches of other "religious seers" with similar experiences. Ellen Harmon is not a *sui generis* case. Those who have been tattooed with a hagiographic depiction of Ellen Harmon may find it virtually impossible to eradicate such tattoos. However, perhaps in viewing parallels with other cases similar to Ellen Harmon's experiences, they will be better able to make a paradigm shift and perceive Ellen G. White as a twelve-year-old Ellen Harmon, torn between feeling condemned to the fires of hell or rapturous that she's bound for heaven via Millerism.

Acknowledgements

THE FOLLOWING INDIVIDUALS HAVE been kind enough to read this manuscript and provide me some oral and/or written feedback: Esdon Bacchus, Scott A. LeMert, James Hamstra, Larry Geraty, Gilbert Valentine, Jonathan Butler, Paul Lee, Calvin Hill, James Hayward, and Douglas Morgan.

We are all tattooed in our cradles with the beliefs of our tribe; the record may seem superficial, but it is indelible.

OLIVER WENDELL HOLMES

INTRODUCTION: *CHILD* OF THE APOCALYPSE, ELLEN HARMON WHITE

Ellen Harmon was, in a very significant religious sense, the spiritual daughter of William Miller. It is sometimes said of a fundamentalist Catholic that "he is more Catholic than the Pope." In a very real sense, Ellen Harmon became more Millerite than Miller. For even after Miller renounced his own erroneous date-setting proclamation, Ellen Harmon still firmly believed that Miller had been divinely guided in his calculations that October 22, 1844 was the exact day of the Second Coming. According to Miller, he had been irresistibly led to this calculation by godly dreams combined with a literal interpretation of fifteen biblical passages. He claimed to have laid aside all traditional commentators and made his calculations based solely on his Bible and a concordance. Thus, when Ellen Harmon encountered him in his preaching engagement from March 11-23, 1840 at Portland, Maine, he completely convinced her that his commonsense, literal interpretation of fifteen biblical passages led to the inevitable conclusion that the Second Coming would occur "about 1843." As a result, the chief burden of Ellen Harmon's First Vision was that the "Midnight Cry," the last phase of the Millerite movement, was divinely inspired. Sadly, Father

Miller's dreams and predictions turned out to be falsified by events. When Christ did not come on October 22, 1844 as predicted, October 23, 1844 marked the Great Disappointment. It might appear likely that this would lead to reconsideration of his purportedly literal method of interpretation. But ironically, a re-examination of Miller's fifteen proof texts demonstrated that Miller actually relied on what Seventh-day Adventist (SDA) apologist F. Nichol himself labelled farfetched and fanciful. Furthermore, Miller's actual method, allegorical-typological-historicism, continued to be utilized by Ellen Harmon and others for their post-Great Disappointment explanations for the delay of the Second Coming. As a result, SDA eschatological apologetics still retain, almost two centuries later, a heavy vestigial burden of falsified Millerite interpretations.

Ellen Harmon encountered William Miller in March 11–23, 1840 when she was only twelve years old, and he was just reaching the zenith of his influential role as Father Miller. In 1909 when asked the date of her conversion, she responded: "Probably in March 1840." William Miller was truly her spiritual Father Miller.[1] Less than six years later she would eclipse him. On November 4, 1826, according to Miller, God had given him a dream commissioning him to warn the world that Christ's Second Coming would occur "about 1843." God also gave him the overpowering divine imperative: "Go and tell it to the world, their blood will I require at thy hand."[2] Following this role model, in 1843 Ellen Harmon became convinced that God had inspired her via dreams as well. He gave her a divine dream, for example, in which the truth of Millerism was symbolized as a temple into which she and the entire world must enter if they wished to escape the cleansing fires of the Second Coming. Then in the winter of 1844–45 Ellen says she had at least two visions. The first vision confirmed that S. S. Snow's Midnight Cry was divine "light" and the second contained a divine command commissioning her as an itinerant prophetess to spread the message of the Midnight Cry throughout New England. Meanwhile, by 1845 Miller had predicted three

---

1. Knight, *Walking with Ellen White*, 101.
2. Knight, *Millennial Fever*, 43–44.

different dates for the end of the world (August 11, 1840; March 21, 1844; October 22, 1844), each of which had failed. Snow had modified Miller's preferred date, March 21, 1844, to October 22, 1844 and this proclamation became known as the Midnight Cry. Its failure was known as the Great Disappointment. With the third "Great" Disappointment, Millerism splintered into spiritual chaos. Ellen Harmon, now armed with divine *dreams, visions, and a prophetic commissioning* of her own, replaced Father Miller as a newly minted prophetess in the shut-door faction of the Disappointed Millerites.

Ellen Harmon was a *child* of the Apocalypse before she morphed into the portly, elderly, Victorian dowager that appears on the cover of Ronald Number's book: *Prophetess of Heath*. Yet most of the twenty million members of the Seventh-day Adventist church that acknowledge her semi-canonical authority never stop to consider that Ellen Harmon was scarcely twelve years old when she had a personal encounter with Father William Miller who became her spiritual guide. Earlier, when only about eight years old, she had continually experienced a morbid, almost obsessive fear of burning in hell. This was exacerbated when, in 1840, an itinerant lay preacher named William Miller announced that the Second Coming would occur by 1843 and the earth cleansed with fire. This terrified Ellen further. Critically, her personal encounter with Miller occurred just after she had to drop out of a women's seminary because her central nervous system remained shattered by an earlier brain trauma. A classmate had struck her full in the face with a rock. She lost consciousness, had been stuporous for three weeks, was reduced to a skeleton, and was not expected to live. When she met Miller in March 1840, she had just dropped out of a women's seminary because of mental incapacity and claimed that she would have died if she had continued. Miller offered her a biblical escape. He claimed that he had discovered fifteen biblical proofs that mathematically demonstrated that by March 21, 1844 the world would cleansed by fire. She only had to believe

Miller's date-setting was biblically based to escape the flames. She believed Miller readily. However, when this date failed, she *still* continued to believe Miller's conclusions were divinely inspired. When March 21, 1844 failed, a follower of Miller's named S. S. Snow said scriptures in Jeremiah, Ezekiel, and Habakkuk *predicted this failure* and a brief "tarrying time." He outdid Miller with even more biblical proofs that the Second Coming would occur after this brief "tarrying time," in a movement entitled the "Midnight Cry." Snow eventually persuaded a reluctant Miller to endorse October 22, 1844 as a new exact date. But Miller and Snow were opposed by ministers who pointed out that Jesus said nobody would know the day or hour of the Second Coming. Nevertheless, Ellen Harmon was completely convinced by the myriad of biblical texts and mathematically exact "prophetic periods" that Miller and Snow offered in support of their assertion that any "sincere" Christian could know the very date of the Second Coming. Reinforcing Miller's credibility, she also claimed she saw in vision that God had given Miller repeated, direct, divine and angelic guidance in his date-setting. In short, Ellen Harmon, between the ages of twelve and sixteen, was convinced that Miller and Snow had demolished the argument that nobody would know the day or the hour. Thus, on June 26, 1842 she was baptized into the Methodist church but, as she always insisted, it was "through Millerism" not Methodism that she found *certainty* of salvation. Another critical model for Ellen Harmon was William Foy, a young, black Millerite preacher who claimed to have visions supporting Miller's date-setting. In March 1844, Ellen Harmon personally witnessed William Foy's ecstatic prostrations *just days prior* to March 21, 1844, the last day of Miller's last year, the Jewish year of 1843 by rabbinic reckoning. Foy was an African-American who preached that the earth would imminently be cleansed by fire. He was so charismatic he attracted thousands. Foy claimed to have had multiple visionary experiences during which he had cardio-pulmonary arrest, as certified by a physician, lasting several hours. Foy's visions and out-of-body experiences provided Ellen Harmon with an impressive role model. During December 1844, she had her First Vision. This vision Ellen interpreted to signify that October 22, 1844 was a divinely preprogrammed date. In 1845, Ellen continued to have regular, ecstatic visionary experiences. These were accompanied by extraordinary (her disciples would say supernatural) physical manifestations—indistinguishable from Foy's.[3] A small group of ex-Millerites, the "Little Flock," which coalesced around Ellen Harmon, claimed that Foy's visionary gift had passed to her.

When Miller's date of March 21, 1844 passed without Christ's Second Coming, S. S. Snow began to eclipse Miller's influence. When Snow's prediction of October 22, 1844 also failed, Millerism experienced total chaos. All the older, mature Millerite authorities had been totally discredited. *Ellen Harmon replaced Miller and Snow*, stepping into the spiritual and emotional void their failed predictions had created. Indeed, Ellen Harmon claimed to have greater authority than Miller, the authority of a prophet. In early 1845 Miller repudiated his own calculations, stating that the Midnight Cry was not a fulfillment of prophecy in any sense. Ellen Harmon claimed that her Little Flock, a designation James and Ellen White gave to their faction of ex-Millerites, was a direct continuation of Millerism. She claimed that Rev 14:6–12 predicted Millerism as the historical embodiment of the first and second angel of Rev 14:6–12, whereas the Millerite faction Ellen Harmon headed was the culminating *third* angel message.

The central focus of Ellen Harmon's visions ever afterward was her insistence that they confirmed the date-setting, Midnight Cry proclamation of October 22, 1844. Even after Miller himself announced that he had been wrong, Ellen Harmon continued to insist that God had led Miller in his dogmas and that his numerous biblical proof texts could not be mistaken. Thus, the SDA church, which Ellen Harmon, James White, and Joseph Bates cofounded, has steadfastly persisted in retaining Miller's allegorical-historicist, proof-texting method. Miller claimed to have based

---

3. As documented below, similar extraordinary physical manifestations and prophetic claims were plausibly made by several other charismatic religious leaders who also shared many of Ellen Harmon's physical, psychological, and sociological attributes.

his predictions solely on his concordance and a Bible. However, this is incorrect. He was very heavily indebted to the allegorical-typological-historicist method, often down to some of its most miniscule and obscure details.[4]

This allegorical-historicist method had blossomed during the Reformation when scores of Protestant commentators had applied wholesale sequences of dates matched to specific verses, especially in apocalyptic passages, culminating in the Second Coming. The cataclysmic Wars of Religion between Catholics and Protestants were interpreted as the final events in the Apocalypse. This method was discredited when its predictions failed, but Miller re-popularized it. At twelve, Ellen Harmon was too immature and ill-educated to have known of *historicism's historical failures*. She was much more impressed by the reams and reams of biblical citations and "prophetic" calculations that Miller espoused. Indeed, her entire social milieu had little acquaintance with and even less respect for "learned clerics" who they considered no better than foppish scoffers. Furthermore, Ellen's New England neighbors were steeped in apocalyptic signs in the heavens as well as prophetic periods and

---

4. There is a striking example of a very obscure but specific interpretation first discussed by Joseph Priestly, and then copied by Miller. On February 28, 1794 Joseph Priestley, (1733-1801), the discoverer of oxygen, made the assertion that the "late revolution in France" was predicted under the symbol of an earthquake in Rev 11:13. Then he adds this minute detail: "And the same hour there was a great earthquake, and the tenth part of the city fell, and in the earthquake were slain of men (or literally, names of men) seven thousand . . . " In short, according to Priestly, the text does not refer to the slaying of seven thousand literal persons. Rather, *seven thousand French titles of nobility were abolished*. William Miller copied Priestley's concept stating: "and in the earthquake were slain of men [names or titles] seven thousand." Uriah Smith copied Priestley's and Miller's interpretation that the slain seven thousand persons really means that seven thousand French titles of nobility were abolished during the French Revolution. For Priestly see Froom, *Prophetic Faith*, 2:746; For Miller see Miller, *Evidence from Scripture*, 106; and for Smith see Smith, *Daniel and the Revelation*, 503, which, quoting Rev 11:13 states: "And in the earthquake were slain of men [margin, names of men, or titles of men] seven thousand. France made war, in her revolution of 1793-98 and onward, on all titles of nobility. It is said by those who have examined the French records, that just seven thousand titles of men were abolished in that revolution." E. G. White, of course, endorsed Uriah Smith's book.

dates. They believed that the northern lights were supernatural signs that had only started appearing in the heavens since 1798, the year which they calculated started the "end times." There was also a popular belief that a 1755 earthquake in Lisbon, Portugal, was the earthquake predicted in Revelation; and that a miraculous Dark Day in 1780 and a meteorite shower in 1833 were additional signs predicted in Revelation.[5]

In short, Ellen Harmon was born into a psycho-social environment which shared Miller's millennialism and inclination to apply his allegorical-historicism to his interpretation of the Apocalypse. Her spiritual brethren were similarly inclined to interpret enthusiastic, ecstatic behaviors, typically accompanying millennial movements, as divine endorsements of their date-setting calculations. Thus, there were two intertwined factors that determined Ellen Harmon's interpretive presumptions. One, a reliance on the method of allegorical-typological-historicism, while imagining it to be a method of commonsense literalism which could predict the Second Coming and an entire sequence of datable events preliminary or in association with it. Two, the subjective conviction that extraordinary, ecstatic Pentecostal experiences were the Holy Spirit's endorsement of a series of chronological calculations culminating in the setting of an exact date for the Second Coming. As a result, the *authority of Ellen Harmon and the validity of the Midnight Cry's date-setting calculations became inextricably intertwined.*

Ellen Harmon was predisposed towards Millerism by factors which probably predated her birth. From the early age of about six to eight Ellen had shown a marked independence of thought and action. Despite being born a twin on November 26, 1827, Ellen Harmon was no duplicate.[6] She was an original from earliest childhood. The words "unconventional," "original," "singular," "self-assured," and "self-contained" only partially capture her essential

---

5. See Jennisken, *Meteorite Showers,* for an authoritative source on the actual history and nature of this meteorite shower. It has regularly occurred for millennia.

6. We are not sure whether she was an identical or fraternal twin.

character.[7] She described herself as being "naturally proud and ambitious."[8]

An incident from her earliest school days illustrates her precocious self-assuredness. When she was perhaps just six to eight years old,[9] she had the following experience:

> I had sat in school with a pupil sitting by my side, when the master sent a ruler to hit that student upon the head, but it hit me, and gave me a wonderful wound. I rose from my seat and left the room. When I left the schoolhouse and was on the way home, he ran after me and said "Ellen, I made a mistake; won't you forgive me?" Said I, "Certainly I will, but where is the mistake?" [He replied the mistake is] "I did not mean to hit you." "But," said I, "it is a mistake that you should hit anybody. I would just as soon have this gash in my forehead as to have another injured."[10]

She marched to the beat of her own drum. Probably she got a great deal of this from her Methodist parents. Her father was a Methodist exhorter. He came from a family of Congregationalists which represented a more sober, if not officially established, church. In contrast, Methodism was what Wigger described as being a "boiling hot religion."[11] Ellen's father apparently was more

---

7. The *EGW Encyclopedia* phrases it this way. Thirteen-year-old Ellen Harmon had an "independent turn of mind" as illustrated by her self-assured and adamant position that her baptism had to be by immersion and not by sprinkling as her "older and wiser" Methodists sisters were pressuring her to accept. See Moon and Kaiser, "Jesus and Scripture," 23.

8. White, *Christian Experience*, 31. Ellen Harmon seemed to model how she presented herself on William Foy. Her earliest books had two main sections: 1) her visions and 2) her Christian experience. She even modeled the title of her book on *Christian Experience of William E. Foy: Together with the Two Visions he Received Jan. and Feb.* 1842. Elsewhere I have documented how she even borrowed a phrase from Foy's visions to describe her own visionary experience.

9. The notorious incident of the rock which struck her nose and almost ended her life occurred afterward when she was nine.

10. Moon and Fortin, "Jesus and Scripture," 20.

11. See Wigger, *Taking Heaven,* 104 for descriptions of visions and ecstatic

drawn to an unconventional, enthusiastic religion and aspired to be a lay leader.

Thus, at a Methodist camp meeting in the summer of 1841 when she was but thirteen, following close on the heels of Miller's Portland, Maine, lecture series of March 1840, Ellen was exposed to "shouting" Methodists who regularly erupted in bursts of ecstatic expostulations, while "taking heaven by storm."[12] This would have a formative effect on Ellen Harmon's expectations concerning both ecstatic behavior and how people were saved. Having "come out" of Congregationalism into Methodism, Ellen's parents and most of her seven siblings were disposed to "come out" of Babylon and Methodism less than a year after Mr. Miller's second preaching tour in Portland, Maine, from June 4–12, 1842.

AURORA BOREALIS OF FEBRUARY 1837, METEORITE SHOWER OF 1833, DARK DAY OF 1780

Her earliest childhood was replete with apocalyptic signs, wonders, slaying in the Holy Spirit, and hell-fire preaching. At age five an awe-inspiring "sign of the end" occurred. As her grandson, Arthur White, documents, the November 15, 1833 *Portland Advertiser* breathlessly reported that "the sky, some say, seemed to be on fire—others add that the stars appeared to be falling."[13] If Ellen was not an eyewitness, she certainly heard about it from awestruck townfolk. This became one of the standard celestial "signs" of the Second Coming which the Millerites believed was due to a direct, miraculous intervention of God which fulfilled a prophecy in the Apocalypse of St. John which speaks of the stars of heaven falling.[14] It is possible that her parents showed the blazing sight

---

experiences common in American Methodism.
12. Wigger, *Taking Heaven*, 104.
13. White, *Ellen G. White*, 19.
14. In 1846, O. R. L. Crosier's pivotal article wherein he proposed an "extended atonement," still cited as miraculous the 1833 meteorite shower and the 1780 Dark Day as proofs that God was "in" Miller's and Snow's date-setting

to Ellen just as they brought Ellen outside to view a stupendous *aurora borealis* about three years later. This, she reported, was when she was still convalescing from her severe brain trauma and her mother had to carry her. Recalled Ellen: "I well remember one night in winter when the snow was on the ground, the heavens were lighted up, the sky looked red and angry, and seemed to open and shut, while the snow looked like blood.[15] The neighbors were very much frightened. Mother took me out of bed in her arms and carried me to the window. I was happy; I thought Jesus was coming. . . . "[16] The *aurora borealis* and various meteorites were touted as "fulfilling the foretold 'Wonders' and 'Signs' (in 'the last days') of Christ's 'coming' and 'kingdom at hand.'" It is noteworthy that the "neighbors were very much frightened." This indicates that the general populace—and not just Ellen—was predisposed to accept Miller's apocalyptic message. They were analogous to prescientific farmworkers who believed eclipses were demonic omens or divine warnings. Millerites insisted that the Northern Lights must be biblical signs of the end because there "appears to be no real ancient history of these phenomena."[17] Henry Jones repeated this erroneous claim elsewhere, citing "wonders in the heavens," "fearful sights," of "blood, and fire, and pillars of smoke." He exhorts: "Let what will be said on the opposite side, the fact will remain that these wonderful phenomena, in their resemblance of 'blood, fire, and pillars of smoke,' have many times perfectly[18] answered to the fulfilling of these prophecies."[19] The editors of the *Signs of*

Midnight Cry. See Burt, "Day-Dawn of Canandaigua, 317-30.

15. Ellen's recollection that the color of the *aurora borealis* was "red and angry" and "like blood" was more subjective than objective because the colors most often associated with the *aurora borealis* are pink, green, yellow, blue, violet, and occasionally orange and white—not blood red. Like Henry Jones cited below, the Bible seemed to require that the *aurora borealis* be a blood red.

16. White and White, *Life Sketches*, 133. For an accessible online version of this book, see https://egwwritings-a.akamaihd.net/pdf/en_LS80.pdf

17. Jones, "Fearful Sights, Great Signs," *Signs of the Times*, 169-77.

18. Millerites almost always described their apocalyptic calculations as "exact" or "perfect."

19. Henry Jones, "Fearful Sights, Great Signs, &c.," *The Midnight Cry*, 178.

the Times insisted that the "bloody appearance of the moon, already spoken of, in February, 1837; . . . ." 2) the Dark Day of May 19, 1780; 3) "Fire and pillars of smoke," predicted by the prophet Joel; 4) what Luke calls "fearful sights and great signs from heaven; 5) and the "*The Aurora Borealis*, or *Northern Lights*, are a *perfect fulfilment* [emphasis added] of this prophecy . . .'" "It is difficult to conceive how a *more perfect fulfilment* of the prophecy could take place [emphasis added]."[20] Thus, it was perfectly predictable that, whether aged five or eight, Ellen Harmon would say when she saw the *aurora borealis*: "I thought Jesus was coming." As these signs made headlines, Ellen's parents may have become aware of "Miller's first published work, a sixty-four-page pamphlet, [which] appeared in 1833."[21]

Young Ellen Harmon was bold, self-assured, and had a razor-sharp sense of moral duty. She was also precocious. In the autumn of 1833, she entered school at age five. Arthur White recounts that she had "great ambitions," and that she "advanced rapidly, and soon the teacher was calling on her to read the lessons for the rest of the class. She moved upstairs with the more advanced pupils, but was sometimes called down to read for the little ones in the primary room."[22] In a word, her scholastic performance was outstanding. She accomplished today's equivalent of skipping a grade, possibly two. She even appears to have become a sort of instructional assistant for the teacher. It seems likely that such outstanding achievement may have earned her the resentment of some of her classmates. She may have even earned the reputation of being a "smart aleck" and "teacher's pet." Ellen suggested no particular motivation for the girl who hit her in the face with a rock, other than that she was "angry at some trifle." A reasonable explanation is that she was jealous and resentful of Ellen and was determined to put her in her place. Ironically, this is what happened. Ellen, who had advanced to the point of being a special assistant to the

---

20. Editors, "Exposition of Matthew, 24th Chapter," 125–28.
21. White, *Ellen G. White*, 19. Ellen White's first book was also sixty-four pages.
22. White, *Ellen G. White*, 25.

less apt pupils, now became a struggling pupil and the girl who had struck her was assigned to help the uncomprehending and now ugly Ellen. A few years later Ellen would term a similar mental affliction as having her mind "locked" so that she could not comprehend Bible arguments. After her injury, she would practically sweat drops of blood but still be unable to comprehend her lessons. Her ambitions for a brilliant academic carrier were dashed. She was forced to drop school.

Even prior to encountering Miller, Ellen was frightened regarding preachers's accounts that the world would shortly end. When she was eight, in 1836, she picked up a newpaper clipping that told of a man in England who was preaching that the "earth would be consumed in about thirty years." Reading newspapers at age eight demonstrated her precocity. She was so spellbound by that paper that she read it to her family. She was then seized with "great terror." It made such an impression on her mind that she "could scarcely sleep for several nights, and prayed continually to be ready when Jesus came."[23] Her morbid obsession with a fiery end of the world preceded her encounter with Miller by four years. To make matters worse, Arthur White recounts that "no pains were spared to indoctrinate" Ellen with "prescribed books for children, and possibly some of the same ones she referred to in later years . . . ." Ellen recalled that she had "read many of the religious biographies of children who had possessed numberless virtues and lived faultless lives." Thus, she "would repeat to herself again and again, 'If that is true, I can never be a Christian.'" "Such thoughts drove her almost to despair."[24] This terrorized response would be repeated both during her personal exposure to Miller's hellfire preaching and her exposure to William Foy who terrified his audiences with vivid descriptions of roiling flames. Foy's live performance, which Ellen Harmon personally witnessed and categorized as remarkable, occurred only about two weeks before Miller's initial prediction of March 21, 1844 for the date when the earth would be cleansed with fire.

23. Moon and Fortin, "Jesus and Scripture," 21.
24. White, *Ellen G. White*, 26.

Millerites believed that signs of the heavens such as a Dark Day of 1780 and the *aurora borealis* were miraculous signs of God's soon arrival to cleanse the earth with fire. Thus, Ellen at age nine was immensely impressed by an *aurora borealis* which occurred on January 25, 1837. Particularly since it had happened just shortly after the disfiguring face wound which she had received from a rock hurled by a classmate. She experienced this as a very close brush with death. This was significant because she was certain she would burn in hell if she were to die.

About two years later when Ellen was only eleven, Miller's prediction that probation would close in 1839 with the collapse of the Ottoman Empire became headline news in Millerite periodicals. In 1831 when Ellen Harmon was only four years old, Miller had predicted the fall of the Ottoman Empire *and the end of the world* for 1839.[25] To this prediction he tied a calculation of another prophetic interval of 1335 years, the end of which was also supposed to result in the Second Coming and the resurrection.[26] Miller stated that "whoever lives until the year 1839 will see the final dissolution of the Turkish Empire, for the sixth trumpet will have finished its sounding." Josiah Litch, one of Miller's chief lieutenants, modified this prediction to foretell the collapse of the Turkish Empire and the end of the world on exactly August 11, 1840. When the Ottoman Empire did not collapse nor the world end, the Millerites reduced their interpretation of the sixth trumpet to an exchange of diplomatic notes, a far cry from the cosmic event initially foretold. Amazingly, Ellen Harmon never abandoned this "exact" fulfillment of prophecy even after it was falsified by events.[27]

Thus, by the time Ellen Harmon was only twelve years old a strong precedent had been set for rationalizing that an "exact" prediction had occurred despite text and history to the contrary. This same phenomenon would repeat itself with Miller's prediction that Jesus would reappear by the last day of the Jewish year 1843, or

25. Rowe, *God's Strange Work*, 134–39.
26. Miller, "Lecture on the Signs," 6.
27. White, *Great Controversy*, 334–35.

March 21, 1844. Scriptures like Hab 2 and Jer 51:45–46[28] were torn out of historic and textual context and reinterpreted to prove that Miller's fifteen proofs were not erroneous but merely "tarrying." By October 23, 1844, Millerites had had to *rejigger three* predictions of the end of the world. They did this *by* formulating *post hoc* explanations reapplying the allegorical-typological-historicist method when history did not fit their previous predictions.

Meanwhile the 1839 to 1840 furor over the Eastern Question had merged into a new phase in Ellen Harmon's personal experience. The injury to her face had forced her to quit her cherished educational goals. Then she attempted to rematriculate at a women's seminary. We do not know the precise dates for this new attempt. However, an estimate that she restarted school in October 1839 would be reasonable. But the attempt was beyond her physical and mental capacities.

CAPACITY OF DEBILITATED TWELVE-YEAR-OLD TO EVALUATE MILLER'S FIFTEEN PROOFS

When Ellen Harmon was first exposed to Miller's personal preaching at Portland, Maine, (March 1840) she had just given up her attempt to resume her education at a women's seminary in the fall of 1839, approximately around the date of her twelfth birthday, November 26, 1839. She had been practically an invalid for between two and three years. Three years earlier, when she was only nine, she was "seriously injured," according to her own account. She had been struck in the face with a rock and had to be carried home. She reported that she had amnesia after the trauma and that she was unconscious for about three weeks. Her mother described this as being "in a stupid state." All her neighbors thought she would die and she wasted away to an almost skeletal state. Evidently, due

---

28. In a series of letters, S. S. Snow reinterpreted Miller's spring calculation for an autumn calculation. See S. S. Snow, "Letter from S. S. Snow," The Midnight Cry, February, 22, 1844; S. S. Snow, "Letter from S. S. Snow," The Midnight Cry, June 27, 1844; and S. S. Snow, "Behold, The Bridegroom Cometh: Go Ye Out to Meet Him," The True Midnight Cry, August 22, 1844.

to being unconscious, she was unable to eat or drink. Ellen states that when she did finally rouse "to consciousness, it seemed to me that I had been asleep." In short, she suffered a very serious brain trauma that she says impacted her "whole life."[29] The mental strain entailed by studies at the women's seminary was beyond her capacity. Ellen Harmon herself flatly stated that had she continued, it would be "at the expense of my life."[30] Roger W. Coon, former associate director of the Ellen G. White Estate, and therefore institutionally inclined to a hagiographical approach to Ellen Harmon's history, stated that Ellen Harmon's "central nervous system [was] shattered" at this time.[31] Given her ongoing debilitated physical and mental condition, when listening to Miller, only three months later in March 1840, *it is questionable if she was mentally capable* of judging the validity of Miller's fifteen proofs during his preaching tour in March 1840.

While Ellen was self-assured and ambitious, she was simultaneously very self-contained and fearful. Secretly she felt unable to live up to sinless perfection, a perfection that she felt was mandatory to reach heaven—like the children in the religious papers she read voraciously. Repeatedly, she describes withholding her fears and struggles from her mother and her twin sister. At Miller's March 1840 revival she felt that she "could never become worthy to be called a child of God." Nevertheless, she stifled her yearning to seek "advice and aid from my Christian friends." During Miller's second speaking tour in June 1842, she despaired because she felt unable to fulfill a duty of public prayer.[32] To pray publicly was the

---

29. Nonetheless, in a manuscript sponsored by the White Estate, an SDA neurologist, Peterson, "Visions or Seizures," claimed that "Ellen suffered minor rather than a severe brain injury." See https://whiteestate.org/legacy/issues-visions-html/#author for an accessible copy.

30. White, *Life Sketches*, 26.

31. Coon, *Great Visions*, 172.

32. See White, "Communications," 20–22 for her recollections of the eleven-year-old Ellen Harmon's spiritual agonies. Her recollections are not always accurate here, however. Nonetheless, I have based my reconstructed timeline mostly on the dates and intervals as she recollected them. Here, she mistakenly dates Miller's first and second lecture tour in Portland, Maine to 1839

first duty, in a series of public duties, which Ellen felt God was demanding of her. With each sequential duty Ellen always hesitated and resisted and then would inevitably feel like she was sinning against the Holy Ghost. When she eventually completed a lesser duty, she would sense a higher requirement, until eventually she was convinced she was called to be a full-blown public prophet. At each step, she doubted her calling and anguish would devastate her. "Despair overwhelmed me, and for three long weeks no ray of light pierced the gloom that encompassed me." "Sometimes for a whole night I would not dare to close my eyes but would wait until my twin sister was fast asleep, then quietly leave my bed and kneel upon the floor, praying silently, with a dumb agony that cannot be described. *The horrors of an eternally burning hell were ever before*

---

and 1841 rather than March 1840 and June 1842. She states that whenever a thunderstorm would pass, she would dare not "close my eyes in sleep, for fear the judgment might come, or the lightning kill me, and I be lost forever." Then she warns her "Dear Young Friends" that the "storm of God's wrath is soon coming upon a guilty world," and that when she was their age, she "was not ready for Christ's coming." Rather, she recalls that she attempted to convince her parents that she was "perfectly indifferent" to religious convictions. "If I was reading my Bible, and my parents would be coming into the room, I would hide it for shame." "The cross of praying in a public meeting was presented" to her. However, why, especially in her religious family, being observed reading the Bible should be an occasion for shame is counter intuitive. Similarly, her desire to appear "perfectly indifferent" to religious themes and why public prayer should be likened to bearing the "cross" of crucifixion is mysterious. Her self-description as a child may shed light on why she felt that her divine commission as Messenger required her to employ multiple nannies for her own children for about thirteen years—beginning when her first child was only ten months old. The American Academy of Pediatrics recommends that infants be exclusively breastfed for about the first six months with continued breastfeeding along with introducing appropriate complementary foods for one year or longer. Ellen G. White obviously weaned her firstborn at least two months short of one year. She stated that she believed that God would allow Satan to kill her firstborn if she did not leave him with nannies so that she could fulfill God's command to be His Messenger. Similarly, with Edson, she had to leave him with a nanny because otherwise God would think she held him as an "idol." See White, *Letters and Manuscripts*, 222–35 for White's perception that her children's illness were attacks by Satan; and that God allowed such attacks to test her to see if her Messenger commission was a higher priority than being a stay-at-home mother to her children.

me [emphasis added]."[33] After returning home from a Millerite revival one evening with her brother Robert, she felt so despairing that she "coveted death" yet paradoxically "feared the Lord would not spare [her] to reach home." She was certain that she would be "eternally lost" and this filled her with "inexpressible terror."[34]

Although in deepest agony for several extended intervals from age twelve to sixteen, Ellen hid her despair. "I concealed my troubled feelings from my family and friends, fearing that they could not understand me." "I locked my secret agony within my heart, and did not seek the advice of experienced Christians...."[35]

Meanwhile she was convicted by Miller's 1840 sermons that "Christ was coming in 1843, only a few short years in the future. The preacher traced down the prophecies with a *keen exactitude* that struck conviction to the hearts of his hearers. *He dwelt upon the prophetic periods,*[36] *and piled up proof to strengthen his position* [emphasis added]." About a dozen of these "prophetic periods" would be forgotten as the disappointed scrambled to explain 1844.[37] Miller's assertion that his multiple exact "prophetic periods" were biblical proofs that Christ would come by March 21, 1844 convinced Ellen to confess to her brother Robert, that she had "not a doubt but that the doctrine preached by Mr. Miller is the truth."[38] Exactitude was a ubiquitous theme in Millerite preaching.

33. White, *Christian Experience*, 16–24.

34. White and White, *Life Sketches*, 138. She and Robert seem to have walked back from the revival meeting alone. Robert lost faith in the Midnight Cry and died very young from tuberculosis in Ellen's lodgings, but not before she was able to reconvert him on his deathbed.

35. White, *Ellen G. White*, 33–34.

36. Ellen Harmon was convinced by Miller's multiple mathematical proofs and "periods." Not merely the single prophetic period of 2300 years.

37. White and White, *Life Sketches*, 137. Ellen G. White asserted that God endorsed the famous 1843 prophetic chart. It incorporated several of Miller's fifteen prophetic periods. This chart included the Seven Times of the Gentiles period from 677 BC to 1843; the 1335-years from 508 to 1843; the 2300-year interval from 457 BC to 1843; the period from 1299 to 1449 (5 months = 150 years); and the 1798 to 1843 period which encapsulated the 1260-year and 1290-year intervals. Only the 2300-year-period would be defended.

38. White and White, *Life Sketches*, 166. Miller's "doctrine" was not the

Every one of Miller's fifteen proofs was "exact." Sometimes exact down to the very hour and not merely the exact day. Miller and S. S. Snow hammered this point relentlessly. They succeeded in convincing Ellen Harmon that so many exact proofs ending on exactly the same year could not possibly be coincidental. Past exact fulfillments of prophecy meant that knowing the *exact day* for the Second Coming was inevitable.

TWELVE-YEAR-OLD ELLEN HARMON'S LACK OF THE ASSURANCE OF SALVATION

Regarding the terror exacerbated by Miller's 1840 preaching, she confessed: "I knew that I must be lost if Christ should come," and her mind was in "great distress." She was especially troubled by her contemporaries' rings, ear-rings, artificial flowers, and costly ribbons. Although she dressed plainly, inwardly she "longed to be sanctified to God. But sanctification was preached in such a manner that I could not understand it and thought that I never could attain to it . . . ."[39]

Ellen Harmon's lack of assurance reflected a typical New Englander's paradigm regarding salvation. Puritan consensus was that assurance could only be aspired to through "sustained zeal, and long and painful introspection." Paradoxically, "assurance itself might be the surest sign that one was not saved." Those with a sense of assurance were most likely simply being deceived by one of the devil's most infamous ruses. "God's wrath was awful, as ministers stressed, and the odds of heaven were slim." "Ministers routinely stressed that the first step to salvation was realizing how thoroughly one deserved damnation." Thus, the typical parishioner was continually haunted by the reality that, as one preacher warned his audience, "you could be approved as godly by the best

---

age-old teaching that Christ would return soon but that he would return by a definite date.

39. White, *Life Sketches*, 27–28. A mathematically certain date was psychologically much more satisfying than the abstract and ethereal theological concepts of justification and sanctification.

Christians and still be merely an unconscious hypocrite heading for damnation." In short, sanctification and a host of good works could not provide assurance of salvation, but lack of it "strongly suggested that [one] was a reprobate and doomed to hell." In the typical Calvinist paradigm, one was forever caught in a vicious catch-22. Whether one felt an assurance or a lack of assurance, one was more likely damned and could only faintly hope for eventual salvation by struggling up a steep, narrow path, like the one Ellen Harmon saw in her First Vision. In contrast, the radically new paradigm of an instantaneous, ecstatic New Birth experience, provided a "settled knowledge [of salvation which] came only through . . . the witness or 'extraordinary seal' of the Spirit . . . ."[40] For Ellen Harmon assurance of salvation seemed the impossible, unattainable dream—until she received an undeniable, direct experience, a *bodily* manifestation of the Spirit.

Describing her mental state in 1841, Ellen proclaimed: "My soul was thirsting for full and free salvation, but I knew not how to obtain it."[41] She experienced "feelings of despair," constantly during 1842. According to standard Methodist practice, members were expected to "methodically" attend class meetings where it was also an expectation for individuals to pray publicly. This requirement so oppressed Ellen that she sank into "deep despair."

The "terror and conviction" brought by Miller's initial Portland appearance had been pervading Ellen Harmon's heart. She said: "The horrors of an eternally burning hell were ever before me." "I dared not die and meet the terrible fate of the sinner." "I frequently remained bowed in prayer nearly all night, groaning and trembling with inexpressible anguish, and a hopelessness that passes all description."[42] She had already heard many preachers expostulating on the terrors, agony, and torments of those damned to hell and now Miller, William Foy, and other Millerite evangelists assured their hearers that unless they accepted the "definite time"

---

40. Winship, *Making Heretics*, 12–27.
41. White, *Spiritual Gifts*, 2:12–15.
42. White, *Christian Experience*, 24.

of October 22, 1844, they too would be "cast out" and perish in eternal darkness. Said Miller:

> But you, O impenitent man or woman, where will you be then?" "*In hell!* O think! *In hell!* a dreadful word! Once more think! *In hell!* lifting up your eyes, being in torment. Stop, sinner think! *In hell!* where shall be weeping, wailing, and gnashing of teeth. Stop, sinner, stop; consider on your latter end. *In hell!* "where the beast and false prophet are, and will be tormented day and night forever and ever [repeated emphasis on italicized *"In hell!"* original].[43]

Furthermore, in Miller's June 1842 lecture series, Ellen Harmon, only fourteen, was totally convinced that he "dealt in plain and startling facts."

PRIMORDIAL PROOFS: 1) "MANY PROOFS" AND "STARTLING FACTS" 2) "TORNADO" OF THE HOLY SPIRIT

In the interval between Miller's first speaking engagement in Portland in March 1840 and his second engagement in June 1842, momentous events had been happening within the movement. During October 1841 the Millerites had held their Third General Conference in Portland, Maine, Ellen's hometown, where she had a front row seat. In May of 1842 the Boston General Conference of Millerites had formally endorsed the doctrine that the Jewish Year of 1843 was the "definite" last year of earth's history. Doubtless, by June 1842 Ellen had been aware of these tremendous events, likely via her intimate connection with Elizabeth Haines, a delegate to the 1841 General Conference.[44] Thirty months later, Ellen says, "While visiting a dear sister in Christ, whose heart was knit with mine, [this same Elizabeth Haines], the first vision was given

---

43. Miller, *Evidence from Scripture*, 104.

44. She had her First Vision while convalescing in the home of Elizabeth Haines; later she had several other visions there as well.

to me."⁴⁵ In early 1845, she experienced a pronounced delirium and multiple visions at the residence of this same "dear sister in Christ, whose heart was knit with mine." After such a long and intimate acquaintance, it is remarkable that Elizabeth Haines was induced by Joseph Turner to write an unflattering account of what Ellen said during her delirious or visionary states. But in the meantime, life-changing developments were happening in her personal life.

BUXTON CAMP MEETING'S ECSTATIC EXPERIENCE FOR THIRTEEN-YEAR-OLD ELLEN

In September of 1841 Ellen had gone to the Methodist camp meeting in Buxton, Maine. She was expecting a "spiritual ecstasy" that would be proof of her acceptance with God, "and I dared not believe myself converted without it." Her expectations were fulfilled. The Holy Spirit was manifest in her face. A "mother in Israel" inquired if she had found Jesus and without waiting for an answer said: "Indeed you have; his peace is with you, I see it in your face!" Thus, temporarily, Ellen felt that she was saved. Her ecstasy at the Buxton camp meeting was so profound that on her journey home the words of ordinary workmen on the streets of Portland came to her as "grateful thanks and glad hosannas"⁴⁶

Given her baptism by the Holy Spirit at the Buxton Camp Meeting, Ellen was accepted as a member of the local Methodist church on probation as of March 22, 1842. On May 23, 1842 she was recommended for baptism. *Then on June 26, 1842, immediately after Miller's second Portland, Maine speaking tour from June 4-12, 1842,*⁴⁷ Ellen Harmon was baptized in Casco Bay, Portland,

---

45. White, *Life Sketches*, 193.

46. White, *Life Sketches*, 23–24.

47 In the initial years of Miller's itinerant evangelism, the various denominations welcomed him precisely because they grew accustomed to baptizing many newly converted persons immediately after his campaigns. When Millerites settled on "definite" date-setting in May 1842, denominations like the Methodists dubbed Miller *persona non grata*. His June 4–12, 1842 campaign in Ellen Harmon's hometown occurred before they could react.

Maine, into the Chestnut Street Methodist Church where John N. Hobart was presiding.[48] This was the largest Methodist church in Maine.[49] Her June 26, 1842 (aged fourteen) baptismal experience reinforced the religious dreams she started receiving. In terms allusive to Christ's baptism she says: "The power of God rested upon me." In multiple ecstatic experiences in the next several months Ellen would typically swoon to the floor, losing all normal human strength. She wrote that the same supernatural phenomenon smote the arresting police when Elder Israel Dammon and she were confronted by arresting officers *circa* February 1845. Similarly, at her baptism she says, "when I arose out of the water my strength was nearly gone, for the power of God rested on me."[50]

Simultaneously with Methodist class meetings, Millerite meetings continued at Casco Street Christian Church, and Ellen was torn between her competing allegiances to Methodism and Millerism.

Ellen concluded that Miller had "substantiated his statements and theories by Scripture as he progressed." Thus, as Arthur White, accurately observes: "Ellen fully accepted Miller's presentations and continued to attend the Advent meetings in the church on Casco Street." Thus, when her allegiance to Methodism and Millerism conflicted, Ellen Harmon would say: "I have not a doubt but that the doctrine preached by Mr. Miller is the truth. What power attends his words, what conviction is carried home to the sinner's heart."[51]

---

48. Pastor Hobart had invited Miller. This date marked the turning of an era. Before this approximate date Millerite preaching was welcomed and resulted in adding many additional members to a miscellany of assorted denominations. But in the summer of 1842 when Millerism officially emphasized date-setting, he became unwelcome. Coincidently, Ellen Harmon's baptism was precisely on the cusp of this inflection point. Although officially baptized into Methodism, she already identified as more Millerite than Methodist. Thus, the following inevitable, existential conflict in her soul.

49. Moon and Fortin, "Jesus and Scripture," 20.

50. White, *Life Sketches*, 19.

51. White, *Ellen G. White*, 38–42. Miller's quintessential, core doctrine was setting a "definite time" for the Second Coming.

Probably, the conflict between Millerism and the church into which she was newly baptized was the source of the "mental anguish" she describes immediately after her description of Miller's June 1842 visit. At Buxton she had the peace of Jesus visible on her face. At her June 1842 baptism she'd had an ecstatic experience. Then her mood becomes gloomy suddenly. She states that: "Despair overwhelmed me, and for three long weeks [sometime July or August 1842?] no ray of light pierced the gloom that encompassed me." "The horrors of an eternally burning hell were ever before me." "I frequently remained bowed in prayer nearly all night, groaning and trembling with inexpressible anguish and a hopelessness that passes all description."[52]

At this critical juncture, she had two life-changing dreams. Ellen Harmon did not consider these dreams to be normal dreams. She believed that they were the first of many future divinely inspired dreams she would recount in future decades. She implicitly interpreted them as the Holy Spirit's divine endorsement of Miller's date-setting theories. The first was a dream of the Temple and the Lamb. The Temple was an obvious symbol for the Millerite Movement. She describes people ridiculing those who entered The Temple, saying there was no danger [of a Second Coming on March 21, 1844], and even restraining persons who were attempting to enter. Those attempting to enter were prospective Millerites. Those who ridiculed and restrained them were the "scoffers" saying that Miller could not possibly know the day or the hour. "Only those who took refuge in that temple [Millerism] would be saved when time should close; all who remained outside would be forever lost."[53] This was a clear premonitory allusion to the door she proclaimed shut as of October 22, 1844. In short, her dreams endorsed Miller's "doctrine" that "time should close" very shortly and those outside the Temple of Millerism "would be forever lost." These "forever lost" corresponded exactly with those in Ellen's First Vision who "rashly denied" the light of the Midnight Cry and fell off the steep path to heaven into the "wicked world below," from

52. White, *Christian Experience*, 24.
53. White, *Christian Experience*, 25.

which they would never be able to remount. Ellen was in the valley of indecision when suddenly the dream ended. Since she had not made an irrevocable decision to leave Methodism and accept Millerism exclusively: "It seemed to me that my doom was fixed; that the Spirit of the Lord had left me, never to return."[54] Thus, she experienced another iteration of divine rejection which foreshadowed her later conviction that if she did not leave Portland and fulfill the divine command to preach her First Vision to the Little Flock of New England, the Holy Spirit would abandon her—exactly as she later said it abandoned Hazen Foss. The second dream, seeing Jesus at the top of a steep stairway, accessed by means of a green cord, saved her. The green cord represented faith in Millerism. In it "a person of beautiful form and countenance" offered to guide her to Jesus but this required her to lay "every treasured trinket" (rings, earrings, bows, and flowers?) outside a door. Then she saw not an angry God but a "Jesus, so lovely and beautiful. His countenance expressed benevolence and majesty." "He then, with a smile, drew near me, and laid his hand upon my head, saying, 'Fear not.' The sound of his sweet voice, caused me to feel a thrill of happiness I never before experienced. I was too full of joy to utter a word. I grew weak, and fell prostrate at his feet ... I thought I was saved in heaven."[55]

ELDER STOCKMAN AND FOURTEEN-YEAR-OLD ELLEN

Immediately after describing her second dream, Ellen Harmon states that she finally came out of her self-imposed isolation and confided, first, in her mother, and second, in Elder Stockman who was preaching Millerism in Portland, Maine. Her choice of Stockman as her spiritual mentor was significant. Ellen strongly felt that she was receiving divine communications via dreams reminiscent of Old Testament prophets. Yet these needed validation and

---

54. White, *Christian Experience*, 26.

55. White, *Spiritual Gifts*, 2:19–20. Compare with Caleb Rich's vision of a benevolent Jesus described below.

interpretation from a kindred spirit. This kindred spirit she and her mother found in the sickly Elder Levi Stockman. He was one of the specific individuals that she envisioned as being in heaven in her first written vision. Like Ellen and her parents, he would be expelled in 1843 from the local Methodist congregation for his uncompromising support of Millerite date-setting. Also, his premature death shortly after denouncing Methodism as Babylon made Stockman the prototype of a faithful martyr for Ellen. About September 1842, only three months after her June 26, 1842 baptism, Stockman validated her growing sense of mission and message by proclaiming that hers was "a most singular experience." Therefore, "Jesus must be preparing you for some special work." Thus, Stockman confirmed that she was a chosen vessel for a "special work." Shortly thereafter Ellen Harmon overcame the next hurdle in becoming God's special messenger. Her duty was to take the first step towards being a public figure by praying in public. Just a few months after Elder Stockman's endorsement of Ellen's special gift, on January 1, 1843, Miller fixed on March 21, 1844 as the date for the Second Coming since it was, according to rabbinic reckoning, the last day of the Jewish year of 1843. For the six-month interval between September 1842 and March 1843, Ellen was a public speaker at various churches, including the Temple Street Church. Partially overlapping this interval, from February 2 to September 2, 1843, five Methodist disciplinary committees were in the process of expelling the Harmons for uncompromisingly advocating date-setting dogmas. Although Miller advocated March 21, 1844, some of his followers asserted that the Second Coming would come even sooner. For example, some said that the Second Coming would occur February 10, 1843 because this would be the forty-fifth anniversary of the February 1798 captivity of the Papacy which marked the beginning of the "time of the end." On December 24, 1842, Joseph Bates, based on his interpretation of the 1290 and 1355 days of Dan 12, predicted that the Second Coming would occur on February 15, 1843, only forty days in the future.[56] Others predicted the Second Coming for April 14, 1843

---

56. Knight, *Joseph Bates*, 64.

because this coincided with the Jewish Passover. Still others predicted the Second Coming for May 1843 since this coincided with Pentecost. We have no stenographer recordings of Ellen Harmon's public proclamations during these months documenting her endorsement of February 10, 1843, of April 14, 1843, or May of 1843 as the date for the Second Coming. However, it is clear that she was absolutely convicted of some "definite time," most likely Miller's March 21, 1844.

FIFTEEN-YEAR-OLD ELLEN'S ASSURANCE OF SALVATION CAME VIA THE MESSAGE OF "DEFINITE TIME."

Ellen Harmon now clashed with her Methodist class leaders who insisted that her positive experience was "through Methodism!" But Ellen insisted that "what Jesus had done for me, [was] *through the belief of the near coming of the Son of God* [emphasis added]." Thus, Ellen Harmon is proclaiming in unconditional terms that *she experienced the assurance of salvation via the preaching of "definite time."*[57] This was a frontal assault on Methodist teaching. In July 1843 Maine Methodists officially denounced Miller's "definite time" dogma as heresy in their Bath Resolutions. Already, during their 1842 General Conference, Millerites proclaimed that "definite time" was a bed-rock principle, a *"Scriptural Test of Saving Faith,"* as Enoch Jacobs entitled his *Midnight Cry!!!* article. Any *genuine* Christian desirous to know *the date* of the Second Coming could and *must know it.*[58] In contrast, non-Millerites, like Lydia Maria Child were not persuaded that knowing the "definite time" constituted "saving faith." She could not envisage a God who had "filled this world with millions of his children [who] would finally consign them all to eternal destruction, except a few [the elite 144,000] who could be induced to believe in very difficult

---

57. It was not the plain, traditional teaching of a premillennial Second Coming that saved. "Definite time" was a compulsory, non-negotiable, "saving faith."

58. Jacobs, "Scriptural Test of Saving Faith," 17–24.

and doubtful explanations of prophecies."⁵⁹ But, of course, Ellen Harmon's First Vision did consign to eternal destruction all those who did not see the light of the Midnight Cry date of October 22, 1844. The Millerite claim to speak of the expectation of the end of the world in 1843 as "the hope within them," said a critic named Luckey, was a "wretchedly perverted use of the Scripture language." "Conversion was sufficient for salvation, and if that were true then belief in '1843' could not also be necessary, as Millerites claimed."⁶⁰ But persons like Ellen Harmon and Mrs. E. J. Marden were most definitively *not* assured of their salvation through typical Methodist conversion experiences. Even after a "second blessing experience," Mrs. Marden felt she had not totally broken away from the "customs of the world." "Then, 'it was plainly shown' to Marden 'that the belief of the immediate coming of Christ was needed to break off the strong attachment of the world.'" Neither justification nor sanctification was sufficient. It was only when I "received the evidence my mind could grasp, that in 1843, I should see Jesus and be made like him" that she had assurance of salvation.⁶¹

FOY'S "ROLLING MOUNTAINS OF FLAME" PARALLELED MILLER'S MESSAGE OF HELL, HELL, HELL

Critically, for her eventual career, at this juncture Ellen was exposed to the mind-blowing, ecstatic experiences and preaching of William Foy. On January 18, 1842 the twenty-three-year-old Foy had a visionary experience at the Twelfth Street Baptist Church in Boston. His symptomology was very similar to that later ascribed to Ellen Harmon. He was "seized as in the agonies of death," lost his breath, and felt his spirit separate from his body which was given an angelic tour of heaven.

---

59. Doan, *Miller Heresy*, 77.
60. Doan, *Miller Heresy*, 117.
61. Doan, *Miller Heresy*, 115–17.

Child of the Apocalypse

A physician, such as they were in this era, testified that he could "not find any appearance of life [in Foy] except around the heart" for two and a half hours.[62] On February 4, 1842 Foy had another out-of-body experience lasting twelve and a half hours.[63] He then went on extended speaking tours to promote the teaching of an imminent Second Advent. It is no coincidence that Foy experienced what he and Ellen Harmon considered were supernatural, divine, physical experiences in *direct connection* with the Millerite proclamation that the date of the Second Coming was known. It is significant that the SDA church hierarchy has accepted Foy as an authentic forerunner of Ellen G. White. This happened despite the fact that Foy's visionary proof that Miller's "definite time" was biblical, turned out to be invalidated. In any case, in January and February 1842, Foy had his two published visions and went on extensive preaching tours just as Miller arrived for his June 4–12, 1842 tour in Portland Maine. It's possible that Ellen Harmon heard Foy in the wintry months of February or March 1842 since she speaks of going to his speaking location by sleigh.[64] But if not then, certainly she was an eyewitness of what she termed his "remarkable" visions during the last weeks of the Jewish year of 1843; namely, early March 1844.

Ellen recounted going by sleigh to frequently witness Foy's remarkable hellfire or heaven messages.[65] She believed that Wil-

---

62. Baker, *Unknown Prophet*, 26, 88–89. His first vision, lasting two and a half hours, was witnessed by Dr. Cummings, Ann Foy, his wife, and eight local citizens. Foy printed signed testimonials from eyewitnesses that Foy was "thrown" into an "apparently inanimate condition" from "some unknown cause." Cummings testified: "I examined him, but could not find any appearance of life, except around his heart." The church where the vision took place was a predominantly Black congregation, located in Southark Street, Boston. The pastor was George Black whom Foy saw in a subsequent vision as if he were in heaven. He had died shortly after Foy's first vision. This paralleled E. G. White's relationship with Elder Stockman whom she saw in heaven.

63. Ellen G. White's longest out-of-body experience was considerably shorter, about four hours.

64. It would be helpful to find and analyze weather conditions during the winters of 1842–44 in Portland, Maine.

65. Baker, "They lived near the bridge," 45–51.

liam Foy had genuine, "remarkable" visions which she inherited, somewhat like Elisha received Elijah's mantle. Foy claimed that he foresaw the earth wrapped in "rolling mountains of flame." He warned doubters in the Midnight Cry that "when the great day of God's wrath comes, there will be no mercy for them" because "they would not believe."[66] This paralleled Ellen White's vision when she was "shown a company who were howling in agony."[67]

In a 2011 reprinting of Foy's visions which is part of the Adventist Pioneer Series, J. N. Loughborough states that "vast crowds" and "thousands" of many denominations invited Foy into their pulpits where he "created a sensation wherever he went" telling his "visions related to the near advent of Christ."[68] Ellen Harmon listened, enraptured, sitting next to Foy's wife, Ann. Another Ellen G. White statement documents that right in the midst of his public preaching of "the day" he was slain prostrate to the floor: "Then another time there was Foy that had had visions. He had had four visions. He was in a large congregation, very large. He fell right to the floor."[69] Such performances made indelible impressions on Ellen Harmon and were a model for her future vocation as Messenger.

MERE DAYS BEFORE MARCH 21, 1844 ELLEN EXPOSED TO FOY'S ECSTATIC HELL-FIRE PREACHING

There was a "Notice" in the *Portland Advertiser*, February 27, 1844, announcing that Foy would be holding meetings at the Casco Street Christian church in Portland, Maine. Given this announcement was at the very end of February, and estimating that Foy preached there about two weeks from March 1–14, 1844, and *given Foy's* preaching that the world would be cleansed by fire *by*

66. Foy, *Christian Experience*, 16–17.
67. Poirier, "Black Forerunner," 17, 25.
68. Foy, *Christian Experience*, 5–7.
69. Baker, *Unknown Prophet*, 123. Note that only the first two visions were published.

March 21, 1844 (as per Miller's chronology), it is easy to see why Ellen Harmon was so convinced that *the Second Advent must occur by March 21, 1844—only one week away!*[70]

When Miller's prediction of March 21, 1844, for the Second Coming failed, almost immediately, dogged efforts to salvage an alternative "definite time" appeared in Millerite literature. The chief spokesperson for recalculating the Second Coming was an ex-atheist, S. S. Snow, who had only recently been converted to Miller's apocalyptic calculations by the apparent mathematical rationality of his fifteen prophetic proofs.

EZEK 12, HAB 2, AND JER 51: SNOW'S PROOFS OF A TARRYING TIME AND MIDNIGHT CRY

Stunningly, Snow claimed that the very failure of Miller's spring date of March 21, 1844 was a success predicted by the Bible. He wrote a series of letters eventually culminating in his August 1844 Midnight Cry proclamation. In this series of letters, Snow succeeded in convincing Ellen Harmon that Ezek 12:22, Hab 2, Jer 51:45–46, and 2 Esd were biblical proofs that supported her belief in the "tarrying" interval of several months beginning on March 22, 1844. His February 22, 1844 letter already argued that the Second Coming was programmed for an *autumn* rather than a *spring* date. This is a typical example of the allegorical-typological-historicist method.[71]

According to Snow's letter of June 27, 1844, Ezek 12:22–24 proved:

> It was necessary that a mistake should be made in regard to the ending of the days, and that this mistake should be general among the expectants of the kingdom, in order that their faith might be tried.... Had not such a mistake been made, there are some prophecies which could

---

70. Burt, *Historical Background*, 15–43.

71. This series of letters included: "Letter from S. S. Snow," *The Midnight Cry*, February 22, 1844; "Letter from S. S. Snow," *The Midnight Cry*, June 27, 1844; and S. S. Snow, "Behold, The Bridegroom Cometh."

never have been completely fulfilled. Such for instance as Ezek. 12:22, "Son of man, what is that proverb that ye have in the land of Israel, saying, The days are prolonged, and every vision faileth?" Also Hab. 2:2,3.[72]

Snow asserted that Ezek 12:22 "could never have been completely fulfilled" without the failed prediction of March 21, 1844. Days would have to be "prolonged" past this date.

Similarly, argued Snow, Jer 51:45-46 specifically refers to the divine "light" in both the 1843 and 1844 message. Claiming that these verses in Jeremiah referred precisely to 1843 and 1844, Snow noted that in the following verse of Jeremiah it stated that

> "a rumor shall both come one year, and after that there shall come in another year a rumor, and violence in the land, ruler against ruler." What is the rumor here spoken of? It is the Advent message.[73] And what is the first year of the message? It is the Jewish year 1843. And God foresaw the passing by[74] of that year of the rumor, he saw it necessary lest the hearts of his people should faint. [75]

"One year" referred to 1843. "Another year" referred to 1844. Then, "there should come another message, and in another year, after the first." Therefore, "the periods could not terminate

---

72. Snow, "Letter from S. S. Snow," June 27, 1844

73. The "rumor" that shall come "one year" alludes to the fact that the Millerites' *allegorical-historicist* interpretation of Jer 51:45-46 asserts that it was fulfilled by the Millerite prediction that Christ would return in 1843. "In another year a rumor" referred to the 1844 phase of the Millerite movement. Ellen G. White and her disciples used the same allegorical-historicist method in interpreting the three angels of Rev 14:6-12 to mean three specific chronological intervals of the Millerite movement. In the 1850-51 Nichols chart designed by Ellen G. White, she asserted that the three angels occupied the specific dates of 1837, 1843, and 1844. See White, *Ellen G. White*, 253-254, 358. James and Ellen White employed the same allegorical-historicist method in interpreting texts referring to the four watches of the night to refer to four specific historical intervals with the fourth watch ending with the Second Coming in October 1845.

74. "Passing by" of the year 1843 is a euphemism for the failed prediction of March 21, 1844.

75 Snow, "Letter from S. S. Snow," June 27, 1844

before the seventh month of the Jewish sacred year in A. D. 1844." Thus, the Jeremiah passage referring to events regarding Babylon in Jeremiah's time are wrested out of context, brought forward over two millennium and marshalled in favor of an exact year and season for the Second Coming: autumn 1844.[76] Snow argued that Miller's failed date of March 21, 1844 was actually divinely predicted by these proof-texts from Ezekiel and Jeremiah. Such embarrassing proof-texts have been almost entirely forgotten by SDA apologists.

Only the most well-known text, Hab 2:3, referring to this "tarrying time" has been retained in standard apologetics. Copying Snow's exegesis of this text, Ellen Harmon, asserted that the "tarrying" vision referred to in Hab 2:3 was the vision of Dan 8:13–14.

Enoch Jacobs, Ellen's first publisher, gave classic expression to this theory:

> The expression, "Though it tarry," supposes time beyond the period when it would be expected to terminate [March 1844]. It however supposes nothing more than a slight error on the part of the expectants, when taken in connexion with the declaration, "IT WILL NOT TARRY."[77]

Thus, Ellen Harmon asserted that God commissioned the Millerites with the divine mandate to predict that the vision of Dan 8:14 was to end on March 21, 1844 for the express purpose that such a prediction would fail. This was to test them to see if they could "wait for it." This "tarrying time" rational for the failure of Christ to come as predicted remains a pivotal point in SDA eschatology because Ellen G. White adopted it and repeatedly referred to it in her allegorical-typological-historicist treatment of Daniel and Revelation.

Such were the *actual*, historical, "biblical" proofs that Snow offered to support his prediction of the October 22, 1844 date for

---

76. Snow, "Letter from S. S. Snow," June 27, 1844.
77. Jacobs, "If the Vision Tarry," 33–40.

the Second Coming. Such were the *multiple, biblical "evidences"* that persuaded Ellen Harmon that God was "in" the Midnight Cry.

FIFTEEN-YEAR-OLD ELLEN INITIATES HER CAREER AS PUBLIC VISIONARY, EVANGELIST, AND SPEAKER

Thus, to resume, possibly in early 1842 Ellen witnessed Foy's visionary exhortations during his initial speaking tour. Shortly afterward, while at her uncle Abner's house, Ellen collapsed on the floor in such a spectacular manner that some feared for her life and wanted to call a physician. However, Ellen's mother assured the small group that it was "the wondrous power of God that prostrated her." Like the prophet Mohammed, several of Ellen's first converts were family members. Ellen confirmed that she had received such a double portion of the Holy Spirit "with such power that I was unable to go home that night." The emerging bud now started to blossom into a visionary career. According to Arthur White, that next evening she "attended a prayer meeting. As she offered her first prayer in public, the burden and agony of soul she so long endured vanished."[78] Then for the next six months she was at perfect peace.[79] Ellen Harmon does not date the exact months

---

78. White, *Christian Experience*, 39.

79. Ellen Harmon also claimed that she now had "clear views now presented to me of the atonement and the work of Christ" See White, *Christian Experience*, 31. This is a critical claim. Later Ellen Harmon will claim that on October 22, 1844 Jesus, *for the first time*, entered into the Most Holy Place as High Priest. However, Miller and other Millerite stalwarts were clearly preaching that Christ as High Priest was already in the Most Holy Place as High Priest—and had been there since his ascension. For example, just one week before the fatidic date, G. Storrs said: "Christ, our great High Priest, has gone *into* the Holy of Holies for us, with his own blood, and 'to them that look for him shall appear the second time without sin unto salvation.' Heb. ix, 28. When he comes out of the Holy of Holies, will it not be on the day typified. Beyond a doubt in my mind it will be." See Storrs, "Go Ye Out to Meet Him," 95. Given Storrs's decisive influence on Ellen and her mother concerning hell, could Ellen have differed from Storrs concerning Christ, the High Priest, in the Most Holy Place? Did she indeed comprehend Heb 9:28?

during which these events happened. However, estimating that it took about two months [July and August 1842] for her to agonize, have the two dreams, and finally consult with her mother and Elder Stockman, the six months would stretch from September 1842 to February 1843. During this time, she again demonstrated her precociousness by beginning an extensive Millerite missionary campaign. Fourteen, then fifteen-year-old Ellen was persistent in evangelizing acquaintances, "some of whom were considerably older than myself, and a few were married persons." Virtually every night during this period she had spiritual dreams; individual cases were presented to her; she received and then imparted spiritual guidance. In effect, she was already God's Messenger or medium.

Ellen's divine insight into "individual cases" is described in virtually identical terms as the prophetic, public prerogatives she would exercise later—from early 1845 to the end of her life. Jerry Moon calculated that Ellen G. White claimed to have had "approximately 2,000 visions," many times more than all the Old and New Testament prophets cumulatively experienced. Thus, her multiple family members noted that she wrote out such "testimonies" compulsively for hours and consigned the care of her four sons to a series of nannies for thirteen years (1848–61) so that she could write and travel. Knight calculated that her two thousand visions resulted in eight thousand letters and five thousand periodical articles. Surrogate, foster parents included the Howland couple, a Clarissa Bonfoey, and Jane Fraser. Ellen's first-born son she left with the Howlands for his first five years starting when he was only ten months old. When Clarissa Bonfoey died, Ellen G. White pleaded desperately with the Louisa Howland to move from the East Coast to Battle Creek, Michigan to become the children's surrogate mother once again. Willie White states that Jane Fraser was his foster mother during his first five years.[80] Ellen G. White's later pattern of having dreams concerning individuals' cases and

---

80. For information on the nannies that the White's employed and how they facilitated Ellen G. White's prophetic writing, speaking, and traveling career, see White, *Letters and Manuscripts*, 216, 301, 308, 468, 492, 637, 645, and 702. Also see Knight, *Walking with Ellen White*, 85, 89–90, 119.

then compulsively writings "testimonies" to such "special cases" began when she was only about fourteen or fifteen years old.

> Night after night in my dreams I seemed to be laboring for the salvation of souls. At such times special cases were presented to my mind,[81] which I afterwards sought out and prayed with.[82]

She believed that special cases were presented to her mind by direct revelation. These were not normal, merely human ruminations. She made such an impression on her elders that she was invited to give a public testimony at The Temple Street church during this interval. According to the *Ellen G. White Encyclopedia*, Ellen was invited to make a public presentation at "a conference meeting of the Freewill Baptists."[83] It may have been Ellen Harmon that the poet Whittier described as

> a pretty miss of "sweet sixteen," or thereabouts, who, commencing in a very low, soft voice, gradually rose to the most piercing treble, as she descanted upon a sort of vision she had had the night before, in which she had seen the awful scenes of the judgment enacted. She was rather pretty and had a very benevolent and mild cast of countenance, which contrasted strangely with the fiendish exultation with which she described the coming agonies of her unbelieving friends and acquaintances.[84]

81. Just so, for decades afterwards, Ellen felt like God was presenting persons' cases to her mind. Then she would give oral counsel and write out hundreds of pages of *Testimonies*. Typically, she would awake around 3 a.m. and write for two-three hours. After breakfast she would resume writing for more hours. July 4, 1859 in a diary entry she wrote: "Wrote nearly all day—important matter." See White, *Letters and Manuscripts*, 637.

82. White and White, *Life Sketches*, 163.

83. Moon and Kaiser, "Jesus and Scripture," 26. Her prophetic predecessor, William Foy, had been converted at age seventeen by Silas Curtis, an ordained Freewill Baptist minister. William Foy was a Freewill Baptist. Thus, Ellen Harmon and William Foy shared religious allies. Given their shared Millerism as well, Foy was a major role model for Ellen Harmon. It is apparent that this "pretty miss," William Miller, William Foy and Ellen Harmon all emphasized the hellish agonies that non-Millerites would endure.

84. Quoted in Hoyt, "We Lifted Up Our Voices," 19–20.

Thus, during this six-month period, Ellen Harmon was making several significant steps towards becoming a public prophet. Meanwhile, major ecclesiological and theological events were occurring. On January 1, 1843, the last year in earth's history was beginning—according to secular reckoning. Meanwhile, on this same date William Miller published an article affirming that the Jewish year of 1843 (March 21, 1843 to March 21, 1844) was the final one in earth's history. At this point Miller was starting to lose control of the Millerite movement. Others, more certain than he about the exact date of the end of the world, were announcing their multiple predicted dates for the Second Coming. Some predicted that February 10, 1843 must be the date of the Parousia because this was exactly forty-five years from the fateful date when the French defeated the Papal forces in Italy, thus officially beginning the "time of the end." Still others announced that April 14, 1843 would see Christ cleanse the earth with fire because this was the date for the Jewish Passover. Yet other proclaimed that May 1843 would dawn on earth's last day because that was the date of Pentecost. The interval of Ellen's entry and exit from Methodism *coincided precisely* with the interval during which Millerism became ever more attached to setting a plethora of exact dates—*all* purportedly with a solid biblical basis.

During this interval Ellen was still attempting to attend both Methodist class meetings and Millerite meetings. But a split was unavoidable. A pastor Hobart, favorable to Millerism, was forced to leave Portland *on June* 30, 1842. "Cox, a pro-Millerite presiding elder in Portland since 1839, was transferred to Orrington, Maine." A Maine Methodist Annual Conference decided to take measures against Millerism in Maine generally. Thus, on February 6, 1843 the Chestnut Street church formed its *first* committee to discipline the Harmons. On March 27 a *second* committee was appointed to discipline the Harmons. Finally, a *third* committee was appointed on April 23, 1843 to discipline the Harmons. On May 1, 1843 an official action was taken to induce missing members to attend Methodist class meetings as required. On May 29 a *fourth* committee of discipline was formed. Then on June 5,

1843 the discipline committee was formed to "keep order" and "prosecute all offenders if necessary." Finally, on August 21, 1843 the Harmons were publicly expelled.[85] Thus, probably sometime between February 6, 1843 and June 5, 1843 Ellen attended her last Methodist class meeting. During this time the class leader and Ellen clashed decidedly on the source of Ellen's sanctification. Ellen credited Millerism for her newly found sanctification. The class leader rebuked her saying: "You received sanctification through Methodism, through Methodism, sister, not through an erroneous theory."[86] Thus, scarcely, *six months* passed between the time Ellen was baptized into the church and the date the first committee was formed *to expel her* for believing in Miller's "erroneous theory." No doubt tension was already building even prior to February 6, 1843. Thus, Ellen never solidified her association with Methodism. She had *entered* Methodism through Miller's preaching of March 1840. She *left* Methodism through Miller's preaching from 1842 onward. Barely prior to the Harmons' final expulsion on August 21, 1843, Fitch preached his famous "Come Out of Babylon" sermon on July 26, 1843.

During the previous six to nine months, Ellen, one elder sister named Sarah (later named Sarah Belden), and her twin sister named Elizabeth banded together to buy Millerite literature from their meager earnings and distribute it without charge to prospective converts to Millerism. This literature contained Miller's, Snow's, and other Millerite preachers's exposition of Miller's fifteen proofs regarding the exact day of the end of the world. Ellen Harmon stressed that Miller always cited biblical texts for his theories while condemning the Methodists who "did not attempt to refer to a single text."[87] She never expressed any doubts as to whether Miller's fifteen proofs made commonsense. Likely, because like Foy, her out-of-body experiences silenced all possible

---

85. See Olson and Coon, "Ellen G. White," 112–14.

86. White, *Christian Experience*, 23–28. Miller's "erroneous theory" was not the classic, orthodox doctrine of the Second Coming, as Ellen Harmon implied, but a date-setting "definite time."

87. White, *Christian Experience*, 44.

doubt. By the summer of 1844 when S. S. Snow promulgated his date-setting Midnight Cry, she'd been slain prostrate in the Spirit numerous times. Ellen G. White emphasizes the fact that she not only had frequent episodes during which she collapsed prostrate, but that she was reproached for this fact. More importantly, she recounts that those who opposed her ecstatic experiences themselves were slain in the Spirit. Thus, they were *divinely compelled* to admit that Ellen Harmon's ecstatic experiences were authentic. In effect, they had to confess that God must be "in" the Midnight Cry and "in" Ellen Harmon. The *authenticity of both Ellen White and the Midnight Cry have been inextricably intertwined* ever since. Such extraordinary bodily confirmations of the proclamation of October 22, 1844 were widespread amongst Ellen Harmon's brethren and sisters. Foy had had an out-of-body experience of heaven. Other Millerites experienced glossolalia, miraculous healings, even twenty-nine-day fasts. Excitement reached a peak in August 1844's Exeter, New Hampshire camp meeting when S. S. Snow proclaimed his Midnight Cry. It seemed to its participants that the Holy Spirit demolished all possible resistance to "definite time," like a tornado. At Exeter, there were meetings that continued "nearly all night, and [were] attended with great excitement, and noise of shouting and clapping of hands, and singular gestures and exercises." Some shouted themselves speechless. "Others had 'literally blistered their hands' through much clapping."[88] Not only did Ellen assert that she "saw" that Miller received angelic and divine guidance in calculating his prophetic charts, she asserted that the "presence of the holy angels was felt" in Beethoven Hall where the Millerites congregated after being expelled from their home churches. Ellen also reported that an Elder Brown, when falling to the floor, had a face "shining with light from the Sun of Righteousness."[89] She was convicted that "power of the Lord was felt upon young, old, and middle-aged." In short, the Holy Spirit was *ubiquitous* in Millerism's Midnight Cry. Additionally,

---

88. Knight, *Millennial Fever*, 177. See also Knight, *Joseph Bates*, 69–70.

89. Is this to be taken literally, as if a supernatural aura similar to the experience of Moses?

under Elder Stockman's preaching of a "definite time," all doubts had been swept away. From Ellen Harmon's perspective the entire date-setting Millerite movement was saturated with the Holy Spirit. Indeed, the very evening she had her interview with Elder Stockman, Ellen Harmon was able to fulfill the duty to pray publicly. Equally significant was the fact that as a result, she had an out-of-body, ecstatic experience: I "lost consciousness of what was passing around me."[90]

In any case, Ellen Harmon says that the twelve months following her expulsion from the Methodist church on September 2, 1843, when her family's expulsion was "sustained" upon appeal, to October 22, 1844, "was the happiest year of my life."[91] But a black cloud was on her horizon.

Ellen Harmon was paradoxically "proud and ambitious," self-assured, independent minded, yet fearful and self-contained. Her soul had been imprinted with an indelible fear of hell and guilt. She was certain that she was quite sinful, yet never enumerated any mortal or even venal sin. When only about nine, she had nearly died of an ugly face-wound that made her loath herself. Thus, she developed an immense yearning for social acceptance and acceptance by an angry God. She felt as if she was not only the "weakest of the weak," but the "ugliest of the ugliest;" that she had a face not even an earthly father could love (or at least recognize) or a heavenly father could forgive. Hell seemed like her inescapable destiny—until Millerism.

IMPRINTING, "TRAIN UP A CHILD" "AS THE TWIG IS BENT THE TREE IS INCLINED"

At critical time periods in her life Ellen Harmon had undergone what the biologist Lorenz termed imprinting. In the Bible it is put more prosaically:

---

90. White and White, *Life Sketches*, 159.
91. White, *Christian Experience*, 51.

Child of the Apocalypse

"Train up a child in the way he should go: and when he is old, he will not depart from it."
Proverbs 22:6, KJV

"Give me a child until he is 7 and I will show you the man."
Aristotle

"As the twig is bent, the tree is inclined."
Alexander Pope

Her entire familial and social milieu was saturated with both religious enthusiasm and millennialism. These experiences were normative and formative for her. A proof-texting, allegorical-typological-historicist biblicism was also the norm in her subculture. It made no difference that Miller's and Snow's key tenet was an extreme date-setting that inverted "no man knoweth" to every sincere Christian must know. It made no difference that Hab 2's vision (written 630 BC) could not possibly refer to the vision of Dan 8:14 (not in existence until at least 553 BC). It made no difference that Jer 51:45–56 could not possibly refer to 1843 and 1844. Or, as S. S. Snow argued: "One year" referred to 1843. "Another year" referred to 1844.[92] Every Millerite sermon with its multiple proof-texts that predicted a specific date for the Second Coming was *supersaturated* with biblical texts and "startling facts" that were "clear and conclusive" to twelve-year-old Ellen. In the introductory section of S. S. Snow's seminal August 22, 1844 True Midnight Cry letter alone, he asserted that numerous texts supported his claim that he knew the exact day of the Second Coming. As scriptural proof of this he cited: 1 Cor 2:2; Dan 7:10; Rom 15:4; Dan 9:25; Mark 1:14, 15; Luke 19:43, 44; 1 Pet 1:9–11; Isa 40:1–5; Acts 17:30, 31; Eccles 3:17; Eccles 8: 5–7; Jer 8:6–9; Hos 9:7–9; and Rom 13:1–14. Though these fourteen texts were quoted verbatim, none of them supported the October 22, 1844 date Snow settled on. Read them yourself. Nonetheless, these texts are the scriptural evidences relied on by Ellen Harmon. Snow cited *many more* texts

---

92. Snow, "Letter from S. S. Snow," June 27, 1844

in the next portion of his letter asserting that the Seven Times of the Gentiles (2520 years) would end, and the millennial Sabbath would begin on October 22, 1844. Snow was unreservedly categorical. He claimed that there could be no doubt that the Second Coming would occur on October 22, 1844. He asserted:

> Our blessed Lord will therefore come, to the astonishment of all them that dwell upon the earth, and to the salvation of those who truly look for him, on the tenth day of the seventh month of the year of jubilee: and that is the present year, 1844. "If they hear not MOSES and the PROPHETS, neither will they be persuaded, although one arose from the dead.[93]

Snow's categorical, uncompromising certainty, his citations of multiple bible verses, his synchronous prophetic periods, all ending on exactly October 22, 1844, completely convinced Ellen Harmon that his date-setting Midnight Cry must be the truth. In December 1844 Ellen Harmon had a visionary experience which she said substantiated Snow's date-setting Midnight Cry as divine light.

Ellen Harmon's conversion *to Millerism* occurred in March 1840, when an extremely incapacitated, fearful, barely twelve-year-old Ellen Harmon was subjected to Miller's fifteen proofs and hell-fire sermons. Just one week before March 21, 1844 Ellen Harmon was subjected to prophet Foy's threats of hell fire should she not accept the higher truth that the Second Coming was due by no later than March 21, 1844. When this date failed, she was subjected to a strained interpretation of Hab 2 that argued that the March 21, 1844 date was predicted to fail. And neither she nor even most Millerite adults had sufficient knowledge of biblical history to understand that the "vision" of Hab 2 (630 BC) could not possibly refer to the "vision" of Dan 8:14 (553 BC) for the simple reason that it was nonexistent until about eight decades in the future.

---

93. Snow, "Behold, The Bridegroom Cometh."

MENTAL CAPACITY

A variety of factors determines whether a person has the legal capacity to participate in various activities. For example, a demented, delirious, or intoxicated person is not considered legally capable of executing a legal contract. A person suffering delusions does not have the capacity to give consent.[94] Every state in the USA specifies a given minimum age for a female to give legal consent for sexual intercourse. An underage female may verbally consent, but if she is underage, the male may be charged with statutory rape. Similarly, there are minimum ages below which neither males nor females may contract a valid marriage. All these legal norms and societal standards are based on the fundamental concept that below a certain age one's mental capacity is not sufficiently developed to make critical decisions. Functional MRIs of the brain have now informed us that a person's prefrontal cortex, a determinative factor in judgment, is not fully developed until the mid-twenties. Certainly, a religious decision conceived of as determining life or death, heaven or hell, must have a minimum age consideration for obvious reasons. Often this is called the age of accountability.[95] Capacity refers to the ability to make a rational decision based upon all relevant facts and considerations. When Ellen Harmon was exposed to William Miller's fifteen proofs in March 1840 at age twelve, she certainly did not have legal capacity to give consent for sexual intercourse or to get married. Did she have "the ability to make a rational decision based upon all relevant facts and considerations"—in regard to heaven or hell? To put it in two other religious contexts: Does a twelve-year-old Jehovah's Witness have

---

94. A delusion is a strongly held belief despite overwhelming evidence that the belief is false.

95. The whole concept of limbo evolved to deal with the perceived dilemma of the eternal fate of an underage person. The rock which struck Ellen Harmon appears to have damaged the anatomical area consistent with a prefrontal cortex injury. Lack of full development of the prefrontal cortex even in the late teens very likely explains the notoriously poor judgment, poor impulse control, and excessive risk-taking behavior of many teenagers that often results in addiction and trauma. See Arain et al., "Maturation of the Adolescent Brain," 449–61.

the legal capacity to refuse blood transfusions? Would a Christian parent consider that their twelve-year-old runaway had the mental capacity to join a Hare Krishna cult in Chicago?

In retrospect, it is clear that the twelve-year-old Ellen Harmon did not have sufficient educational background, did not have sufficient knowledge of the Scriptures, and did not have sufficient development of her prefrontal cortex to make a balanced assessment regarding Miller's fifteen proofs.[96]

Sociologically, Millerites were being shunned by their non-Millerite neighbors. Reciprocally, Millerites denied the validity of non-Millerite *views and sincerity*. As a result, Millerites inured themselves against any of what they branded "obsequious bigotry, or the most unpardonable ignorance."[97] The growing criticism the Millerites received for date-setting resulted in them becoming *ever more resistant* to reasonable critics whom Ellen Harmon branded as the "Synagogue of Satan" in her First Vision.

If one studies the many leading Millerites' post-Disappointment "Afterlife," their staggering feats of cognitive dissonance are flabbergasting—and they were adults. The previously rational atheist, S. S. Snow, soon fancied himself as Elijah. Ellen Harmon's publisher, Enoch Jacobs, became a sexless Shaker. Multiple other rank-and-file adult Millerites engaged in practically every species of fanaticism; most based on a "spiritualizing" of the Second Coming.[98]

---

96. Nichol, *The Midnight Cry*, 507–10 and "Appendix L" characterized these proofs as "farfetched" and "fanciful," and he was the dean of SDA apologists who wrote the classic defense of *The Midnight Cry*. F. D. Nichol had sufficient capacity to recognize that Miller's fifteen proofs were "farfetched." The twelve-year-old with a severe brain injury, Ellen Harmon, did not. Nor did her total immersion in Millerite enthusiasm from age twelve to sixteen result in any improved capacity.

97. Hale, *Second Advent Manual*, 7, 30.

98 All the significant adults in her life, her parents, Elizabeth Haines, Elder Stockman, Brother Fitch, Father Pearson and his sons, were fervent members of a small, isolated minority which perceived itself as being persecuted and was perceived by outsiders as an extremist cult, particularly during the "Come Out of Babylon" phase. This tended to make committed members of the Millerite movement hold even more tenaciously to their convictions—just like Jehovah's

There is one obvious source for these peculiar ideas: The preaching of a false-species of allegorical-typological-historicism and its inherent date-setting. Once this speculation imploded, its adherents had already burnt all their exegetical bridges. Once it was obvious that the date-setting Midnight Cry had been falsified by events, persons were desperate to find some coherent alternative. They had run into a biblical and spiritual dead-ended box canyon and now were climbing the walls.

Ellen Harmon was suffering along with the rest. A little appreciated fact about Ellen during the interval between the Great Disappointment and her first missionary voyage to Poland, Maine is that she convalesced with Elizabeth Haines for several imprecisely known intervals. The *Ellen G. White Encyclopedia* states that Elizabeth Haines "opened her home to teenage Ellen Harmon during her times of illness." Perhaps she had even cared for Ellen, aged nine, when she had been struck in the face with a rock. Perhaps she had also cared for Ellen, aged twelve, when she dropped out of school, (the female seminary), once more. In any case, she was evidently a personage of some prominence because it also says that Haines was "listed as a delegate with Orinda Haines at the third Millerite General Conference held in Portland, Maine, during October 1841."[99] That Ellen's parents were intimate enough with the Haines family to have Elizabeth Haines care for her after the Great Disappointment when Ellen seemed on death's door, suggests that Ellen likely absorbed the latest and most important news about Millerism during critical phases of its development through the Haines family. She stayed at the Elizabeth Haines home in November and December 1844 immediately after the Great Disappointment. Her health so deteriorated (from the most happy year of her life) to nearly being on her death-bed.[100] She claimed that she had

---

Witnesses will insist that their children not receive blood donations despite life threatening illnesses. Those in the minority group are particularly unable to accept any reality checks from "persecuting" outsiders. See also Gilbert Valentine's recent biography on J. N. Andrews for amazing displays of fanaticism.

99. Similarly, Joseph Bates was a delegate to another Millerite General Conference.

100. By October 22, 1844 Ellen Harmon was so committed to 1) what she

her First Vision at Elizabeth Haines house in December 1844. The *Ellen G. White Encyclopedia* also documents that several

> significant visions occurred in the Haines home during 1845. It was in this home that Ellen received a vision that rebuked Joseph Turner for using mesmerism. In the spring of 1845, it was also in Haines' home that Ellen had her "new earth" vision . . . . After this vision Haines cared for Ellen in her home for two weeks during a bout with illness. During her illness *Ellen experienced mental confusion* [emphasis added].[101]

The *Ellen G. White Encyclopedia* goes on to describe that Ellen Harmon made some inappropriate remarks "during her delirium." The exact date of this episode is unknown. Probably it occurred around April 1845, the date many shut-door advocates had proclaimed for the Second Coming. In 1859 Ellen G. White states that it occurred after her return to Portland, Maine from Orrington where opponents were hunting her. When they found that Ellen had escaped, they whipped the accomplices that helped her escape. She described her delirium as having been caused by a conflict with Joseph Turner. He attempted to turn her friends "and even my relatives against me, and he succeeded in a measure." Thereafter, she "sank in discouragement, and *my mind wandered for two weeks* [emphasis added]. My relatives thought I could not live." When her mind "wandered for two weeks" is reminiscent of the stuporous state that she was in for three weeks after her brain injury.[102] However, this episode of delirium, or "mental confusion," posed only a temporary setback for Ellen Harmon. With her first written vision, she had now entered a new phase in her career as God's Messenger. But how did Ellen Harmon's spiritual brethren

---

believed to be "clear and conclusive" biblical proofs, and 2) the proofs being validated by being slain prostate in the Holy Spirit, that she found it impossible to envision the possibility that Millerite presumptions and proofs were faulty.

101. Burt, "Elizabeth Haines," 393–94. The written account of this vision did not appear until much later on January 24, 1846 in the *Day Star*.

102. White, *Ellen G. White Letters and Manuscripts*, 765–66.

distinguish between her "delirium," her "mental confusion," and her out-of-body ecstatic visions?

Actually, her career as God's visionary Messenger predated her December 1844 First Vision. Already from about September 2, 1843 (expulsion from Methodist church) to March 21, 1844 (the little disappointment), she had felt "called" to give her testimony.

She felt like God's Spirit was frequently, very noticeably manifest in meetings with Adventists who had also come out of Babylon [Methodism], but after about six months some who "had come out from the formal churches" disbelieved in her experience and she herself started to doubt it and "withheld my testimony for fear of offending my brethren."[103]

Despite their position on the fringe, the Millerite leadership attempted to maintain a modicum of respectability. William Miller and J. V. Himes rejected visionaries and stressed *sola scriptura*. They most especially did not want to be charged that the movement depended on modern prophets. There was a consensus that direct, prophetic revelations ended about AD 95 with St. John's Revelation. They were well aware that assorted prophets, like the French Prophets[104] and Mormon prophet, had brought disrepute

---

103 White, *Spiritual Gifts*, 2:26.

104. With the revocation of the Edict of Nantes in 1685, the French monarchy began vigorously persecuting the Protestant Huguenots. In reaction to this, Huguenot children, as young as six months to three years old, displayed what their supporters claimed were supernatural gifts of prophecy. They predicted the future, spoke in perfect French, (although this was not their native tongue), had "agitations" of their entire bodies, exhibited supernatural strength, and quoted lengthy passages of scripture. Mary Rouvierre reported a three-year-old that said: "I see the heavens open, and my God discloses to me his glory!" It was claimed that this fulfilled Matt 21:16, KJV: "Out of the mouths of babes and sucklings thou hast perfect praise." The physical feats of supernatural strength, the displays of the gift of prophecy, the claims of seeing the heavens opened, and the very young age of the French prophets all have parallels to Ellen Harmon's characteristics. See Misson, *A Cry from the Desart*. See also Walters, *Child Prophets of the Huguenots*. Therein are recounted the tales of an Isabeau Vincent, fifteen, who "spoke with her eyes closed, commented on the Bible and called sinners to repent." "Nine month old babies prophesied in their crib." Child prophets "said they saw the open Heaven, angels, paradise, and hell." Another young prophetess "quoted the Old Testament and the New

onto the "gift" of prophecy. Thus, even those who had "come out of Babylon" had a strong presumption that Ellen Harmon's "testimony" should not guide them. Amongst Ellen's disciples, this caution and inhibition broke down in 1845, particularly after the Albany Conference. Meanwhile, Ellen's reticence in the face of her social milieu's hesitancy, made her "sensible that the Spirit of God was grieved." By this time Ellen was resolute enough to overcome such hesitancy and she advanced from merely offering public prayer to being an exhorter. For about thirteen months prior to her First Vision, she was already receiving special visitations of the Holy Spirit which gave her a "testimony" which she felt obligated to make public. When she shrunk from this, she concluded that she had grieved God.

Then a dramatic event convinced Ellen's skeptical brethren that "it was the Spirit of God that was upon" her. The very person from a family most opposed to her prostrations fell "like one dead" and when resuscitated, praised God, implicitly endorsing Ellen Harmon's experience. This set off a domino reaction. Another doubter from the same family also "had no faith that it was the Spirit of God that was upon me." He challenged her, asserting that God would have more likely chosen an older, godlier person. But that very person was "immediately prostrated" and when recovered "declared it was of God." Then the very person who most doubted her, also "fell prostrate to the floor." Afterward, "he confessed he had done wrong in opposing me." Ellen's father also verified that the entire opposing family "were prostrated by the power of God." Said Ellen Harmon: "They regretted that they had opposed me, and confessed their error."[105] Consequently, "the Spirit of the Lord

---

Testament as if she knew the whole Bible by heart. She illustrated passages with such accuracy that everyone was dumbfounded." A brother Clary proved his prophetic credentials by putting himself in an *auto da fé*. "Someone lit it and the flames were higher than his head. When the flames died down, Clary got out unharmed, without even the smell of smoke in his hair or clothes."

105. The moral of the story is that all others who doubted and opposed Ellen should confess their error also.

often rested upon me in great measure. . . . I expected Jesus to come and make me immortal [emphasis added]."[106]

In this manner, Ellen became convinced that the "Spirit of the Lord" was giving her visionary experiences confirming Miller's and Snow's date-setting message. She asserted her authority to confirm who else God had endorsed. In addition to putting her seal of approval on Miller's and Snow's calculations, in 1846 she would claim that she had visions proving that O. R. L. Crosier had been "given the true light" concerning the "extended atonement" and the sanctuary.

In short, Ellen and her local Millerite community were in the process of becoming convinced that God was *physically* endorsing Ellen's authoritative visionary claims. Ellen Harmon describes the Holy Spirit's action in prostrating her opponents much like she described the Holy Spirit's action in prostrating (multiple times) the forces arresting Israel Dammon, rendering them unable to move him.[107] In other words, even before December 1844 she is establishing herself as a spiritual authority who is not to be toyed with.

For approximately twelve to fourteen months prior to October 22, 1844 Ellen Harmon frequently had ecstatic, visionary experiences. And these visions, *like Foy's*, convinced Ellen Harmon that the Second Coming was due by October 22, 1844. As she herself stated, "I expected Jesus to come and make me immortal." She made no record that "the Spirit of the Lord" ever cautioned her not to believe in a specific date.[108] Why not? Unlike her December 1844 First Vision, God never instructed her to write out her pre-December 1844 visionary experiences. She never reported a vision warning her that it was presumptuous and unbiblical to predict a precise date.[109] In fact, it was not until her second (written) vision

106. White, *Spiritual Gifts*, 2: 26–29.
107. Hoyt, "Trial of Elder I. Dammon," 29–36.
108. Although James White later said that Ellen Harmon did give just such a caution a few days prior to the new date he was championing in the fall of 1845. Even then she let him vigorously promote the new exact date in writing for almost a year until only about three weeks prior to the new exact date.
109. Oddly, despite the fact that Ellen Harmon claimed that God gave her frequent ecstatic visions prior to October 22, 1844 and that God sent frequent,

about a week afterwards that Ellen was instructed that she must travel outside her own circumscribed Portland community. As yet, she had not received the corporate calling of the Little Flock. This would occur under the leadership of Father Pearson, from the same Pearson family that published the visions of William Foy and introduced her to James White.

Ellen Harmon was well acquainted with Millerite literature and Miller's fifteen proofs. She describes a period of about a year prior to October 22, 1844 during which she, her older sister Sarah, and her twin sister Elizabeth scrimped their misery earnings to buy Millerite "books and tracts to be distributed gratuitously."[110]

Meanwhile, in addition to her extensive and intensive, one-on-one missionary work with acquaintances, Ellen Harmon was becoming a local celebrity. James White recalls observing sixteen-year-old Ellen Harmon during the summer at Portland in 1844. He reported that "her experience was so rich and her testimony so powerful that ministers and *leading men* of *different churches* sought her labors as an exhorter in their *several* [emphasis added] congregations."[111] "Typically, a [Methodist] preacher's career followed a progression from class leader, to exhorter, to local preacher, to itinerant preacher."[112] Her father had long fulfilled the role of exhorter in the Methodist church. In a significant sense Ellen Harmon first superseded her biological father as exhorter, and shortly afterward *she replaced her spiritual father, William Miller, as God's special messenger*. Her rapid rise in status was eventually ratified by the Portland, Maine Millerite "church" parish under the leadership of Father John Pearson. She would very shortly reach the pinnacle of "itinerant preacher" when the Father Pearson group endorsed her call to evangelize outside of Portland, Maine. This

---

divine, angelic guidance to William Miller prior to October 22, 1844, in neither case did God correct their mistaken conviction that the Second Advent would occur exactly on October 22, 1844. Neither did William Foy receive such a caution.

110. Ellen G. White, *Christian Experience*, 38–40.
111. White and E. White, *Life Sketches*, 126.
112. Wigger, *Taking Heaven by Storm*, 29–31.

was significant. This meant that a local Millerite faction renounced the national Millerite authority, including William Miller and J. V. Himes who explicitly denounced contemporary prophets. Meanwhile, she was a public speaker in Portland, Maine for over a year prior to December 1844's vision. It was such public labors which established the foundation of Ellen Harmon's credibility as a later shut-door leader. This, and her numerous personal converts due to her one-on-one ministry, resulted in the prompt reaction of many Portland Millerites when she promulgated her First Vision. Her prophetic claims were immediately accepted. This description of Ellen Harmon is at odds with the usual modern perception of her in which it is imagined that she rocketed from total obscurity on October 21, 1844 to public prophetess by January 1, 1845.

Ellen Harmon progressed through several phases of spiritual development. In her initial phase she was a tormented prepubescent in a Calvinistic tradition tortured by the twin agonies of the predestination of an eternally burning hell and the exigencies of living a perfect life of sanctification. She inherited a moralistic library of perfect childhood examples and felt she could never live up to their examples. Though never mentioning either any venal or mortal sins, other than perhaps inordinate ambition, she was certain she was condemned to hell should she die before reaching home one night from a Millerite revival. She did not consider herself worthy of the title Christian. She sought to transcend this obstacle simultaneously through Methodism and Millerism. Paradoxically, the inspiration she received through Miller in 1840 helped her become a Methodist, but the justification and sanctification of Methodism gave her but ephemeral relief. An integral part of her Methodist heritage also taught her that she had a duty to pray publicly. Her reticence to pray publicly convinced her that she was still condemned to hell. Praying publicly was merely her initial step to becoming a corporate spiritual leader. In the Methodist ecclesiological hierarchy there were the following levels. The entry level consisted of being an lay exhorter. The intermediate level was being a local pastor. The highest level was being an itinerant minister.[113] Ellen could express her newly found assurance of salvation by praying publicly. But no sooner had she progressed this far than the duty to exhort others seemed to impose itself. In the Methodist tradition, not every parishioner had the duty to exhort. However, Ellen Harmon did not experience this as an option but as a *divine command*. Again, she felt estranged from God unless she consented to fulfill this higher duty. She only escaped another "dark night of the soul" by acting in this capacity. The following stage was becoming a kind of local evangelist. In this capacity she engaged in both one-on-one ministry as well as local public speaking. But then she reached the highest stage, that of an itinerant minister. Here again, she was certain that she was abandoned by God and eternally lost (or was it that she had abandoned God?) until she accepted that divine command. This became possible only through the Little Flock presided over by Father Pearson about January 1845. Even after affirming her role of prophetess publicly and in actual practice, she was beset by doubts. On such occasions she felt consigned to outer darkness and was ritually struck dumb. She goes to some trouble to describe these stations of the cross. She earnestly desires that her readers will understand that each step on her way to becoming a public, itinerant prophetess was an unconditional, *divine imperative*. Without accepting the mantle of prophetess, she would be like a Hazen Foss, cast out into outer darkness forever.

Ellen Harmon's initial lack of assurance reflected a typical New Englander's paradigm regarding salvation. The experiences of Richard Randel, Freewill Baptist founder, and Caleb Rich, Universalist trailblazer, were remarkably similar to Ellen Harmon's own prepubescent spiritual struggles. Their spiritual agonies and eventual divine callings shed a comparative light on Ellen Harmon's experience.

---

113. The socio-religious norms of this era considered that it was as appropriate for a woman to be a "pastor" as the Catholic Church today considers it appropriate that a woman be a priest. But a direct baptism by the Holy Spirit and the consequent out-of-body experience could still consecrate a woman as a prophetess.

Both these men asserted that the Lamb of God revealed himself *directly* to them during ecstatic experiences. These ecstatic states included what they believed to be supranatural physical signs like those manifested by Ellen Harmon and William Foy. They too would establish new denominations with distinctive new doctrines which they also asserted were of divine origin. They claimed not to be "taught by man." God had given them direct revelations which proved their teaching had divine origins.

CALEB RICH, UNIVERSALIST VISIONARY

Caleb Rich, born in Massachusetts in 1750, "the most important native New England Universalist leader," like Ellen Harmon, had a number of visionary experiences which confirmed his particular mixture of theological ideas.[114] After one particularly intense vision, he enunciated universal salvation for all mankind in the most radical way. Thus, in words almost exactly like Ellen Harmon's, he asserted:

> I could say in truth that the gospel that was preached by me, was not after man; for I neither received it of man, *neither was I taught it by man*,[115] but by the revelation of Jesus Christ [emphasis added], through the medium of the Holy Spirit in opening my understanding to understand the scriptures.[116]

He came to this radical conclusion after a tumultuous spiritual journey. He, like Ellen Harmon, was very disturbed by the idea of souls burning in hell. He was born into a clan that believed

---

114 Marini, *Radical Sects*, 72–75.

115. Note Ellen Harmon's virtually identical phrase: "I know the light I received came from God, it was not taught me by man. I knew not how to write so that others could read it till God gave me my visions" See White, *Ellen G. White*, 128. Both Rich's and White's claims were likely modeled on Paul's apostolic claim from Gal 1:12 KJV: "For I neither received it of man, neither was I taught it, but by the revelation of Jesus Christ." Paul is claiming direct revelation from the risen Christ. White and Rich are asserting a similar authority.

116. Marini, *Radical Sects*, 72–75.

in Calvinistic predestination; that is, only the elect were chosen for salvation, while the remainder of humanity was destined for hell. Like Ellen Harmon, who was deeply disturbed when her mother suggested to her that sinners would not burn in hell eternally, he shared the common belief that the terrors of hell were necessary to frighten sinners into repentance. Furthermore, disbelief in the existence of hell was a mortal sin which would put him in danger of that very hell which so perturbed him. In 1772, in a state of extreme emotional distress, suddenly, "I saw a vision." A "celestial guide" appeared which revealed to Rich an incomplete stone wall and informed him that he was the very stone to complete that wall; a stone "placed by unerring wisdom into God's building before the foundation of the world." Then in a second "vision of the night," a "celestial friend," instructed him to abandon his previous religious ideas and associations, and to come out of Babylon. Rich arrived at a mountain summit, "the house of God and gate of heaven," (like Bethel to Jacob), then awoke and immediately received, (like the fifty texts E. G. White received), a number of scriptural texts verifying that his vision was "an outpouring of the spirit of God." Thus, he understood that Christ's redemption was universal, there was no hell or "endless misery" for unregenerate sinners.

In 1778, he had further decisive charismatic episodes. In one he saw a luminous personage enter his house and expound on Hagar and Sarah. He was shown that the differences between the two were superficial; that his previous concept that the "Hagars" were damned to extinction while the "Sarahs" were predestined to heaven was false; that all existent churches had corrupt beliefs; and that the Second Coming was fast approaching. The visitor then anointed him messenger (like EGW) and announced that he had a call "to proclaim the same gospel." This was confirmed the next day when, while meditating, he suddenly "felt as it were a shock of electricity, my lips quivered, my flesh trembled, and felt a tremor throughout my whole frame for several days, which was noticed by my wife." A second confirmation occurred in a "vision of the night" in which Rich was visited by "Jesus the Christ of God" himself. This vision has remarkable similarities with Ellen Harmon's second dream of Jesus. Ellen said: "I stood before Jesus. There was no mistaking that beautiful countenance; that expression of benevolence and majesty could belong to no other . . . . I was too joyful to utter a word, but overcome with emotion, sank prostrate at His feet."[117] Caleb Rich said:

> The Lord was a "beautiful personage" possessed of "an unspeakable grace, mercy, meekness, mildness, loving kindness, gentleness, and compassion" that "beamed in his countenance." Christ conversed "with the sociability of an equal, and all that tenderness and pity of a tender mother to a young child." He gave Rich "two small portions of food resembling corn" and said, "Eat sufficiently of it thyself; and of it feed my sheep and lambs, and it will never exhaust, it will be sufficient for thee at all times."[118]

Whether or not there was an external, objective reality to any of Rich's visionary experiences, they inspired him to establish a mass movement called universalism. Its unique core doctrine was revealed during his visionary experience: [119] Salvation was universal; no one would burn in hell.

RICHARD RANDEL, FREEWILL BAPTIST FOUNDER

Richard Randel was the founder of the Freewill Baptists.[120] He was born 1749. In 1770, He initially thought that Whitefield, the Grand Itinerant was a "worthless, noisy fellow." But upon learning of the Itinerant's death, he was struck by "an arrow from the

---

117. White, *Christian Experience*, 27.
118. Marini, *Radical Sects*, 72–75.
119. Ellen Harmon's First Vision led to the unique SDA doctrines that October 22, 1844 was a date of historic and salvific importance; that the Millerite movement was the historic fulfillment of Rev 14:6-12's three angels's messages; and that Midnight Cry was a non-negotiable truth, eventually blossoming into the doctrine of the Investigative Judgment. Anybody "rashly" denying it would fall off the steep, narrow path to heaven and find it impossible to remount.
120. Ellen Harmon's forerunner, William Foy, was a Freewill Baptist.

quiver of the Almighty." He was convicted that "Whitefield is now in heaven, while I am in the road to hell." Like young Ellen Harmon, he continued in "unutterable horror more than three weeks," despairing "of obtaining salvation from any, or all of my former religious duties." He was rebaptized into the Baptist church in 1776 and became an itinerant licentiate of the Madbury Baptist Church, sparking a revival in 1777. His "New Light" message was opposed by more staid "Old Light" authorities. Initially his Arminianism was not an issue, but soon Baptist elders of the region quizzed him on the doctrines of predestination and election which he neither understood nor believed. He had to withdraw from the pulpit and so retired to his farm for a retreat in which "he cried constantly to the Lord to be taught" and given the correct dogmas on these questions. He became convinced that he was excessively bound by traditions. When he yielded to the Holy Spirit, he exclaimed: "O! the flaming power, which instantly passed through my soul . . . I had no feeling of any thing, but the great and awful, terrible and dreadful majesty of God . . . ." He was put into a state in which: "I never could tell whether I was in the body or not." He then had aural and visual impressions. "I saw a white robe brought down and put over me which covered me, and I appeared as white as snow." A Bible appeared which held the key to all his theological questions. "I saw that [the Scripture] ran in perfect connection with the universal love of God to men—the universal atonement, the work of redemption by Jesus Christ . . .—the universal appearance of grace to all men." These anti-Calvinist beliefs were confirmed by "the personal experience of the Spirit." When he returned to consciousness, "all flowing with sweat, and was so weak I could hardly stand up," he calculated that he'd been in a trance state for one and a half hours. He then led conferences in which "freewill principles" were expounded. By 1800 his distinctive message had grown "into the [New England's] hill country's largest indigenous religion."[121]

Caleb Rich, Richard Randel, William Foy, and Ellen Harmon all went through agonizing spiritual struggles while seeking assurance of salvation. All then had dreams and/or visions which

---

121. Marini, *Radical Sects*, 63–67.

solidified their personal assurance but more importantly convicted them of unique doctrinal dogmas. Because they were convicted that they had received such doctrines during personal visionary experiences with Christ, they were certain that these doctrines were eternal truths. The dogmas that they had received during their encounters with God's Spirit were not "taught them by men" but were direct revelations.

FATHER PEARSON AND PORTLAND CHURCH RATIFY ELLEN'S DIVINE CALL

Prior to the collapse of the Midnight Cry on October 22, 1844, Ellen Harmon had already become an influential voice—giving her testimony at several churches at the behest of leading ministers.

Many others in the Millerite movement had ecstatic experiences during which they collapsed, prostrated on the floor, "slain by the Holy Spirit." But Ellen Harmon was destined to transcend these experiences and be anointed a special Messenger of the Lord. The saintly Elder Stockman confirmed that her visionary role was special. Jesus was preparing her, like the child Samuel, "for some special work." Yet despite repeated ecstatic experiences, after the Great Disappointment, Ellen descended into extreme depression.

> I coveted death as a release from the responsibilities that were crowding upon me. At length the sweet peace I had so long enjoyed left me, and despair again pressed upon my soul.
>
> The company of believers in Portland were ignorant concerning the exercises of my mind that had brought me into this state of despondency; but they knew that for some reason my mind had become depressed, and they felt that this was sinful on my part, considering the gracious manner in which the Lord had manifested Himself to me. Meetings were held at my father's house, but my distress of mind was so great that I did not attend them for some time. My burden grew heavier until the agony of my spirit seemed more than I could bear. At length I was induced to be present at one of the meetings in my

own home. The church made my case a special subject of prayer. Father Pearson, who in my earlier experience had opposed the manifestations of the power of God upon me, now prayed earnestly for me, and counseled me to surrender my will to the will of the Lord. Like a tender father he tried to encourage and comfort me, bidding me believe I was not forsaken by the Friend of sinners.

I felt too weak and despondent to make any special effort for myself, but my heart united with the petitions of my friends. I cared little now for the opposition of the world, and felt willing to make every sacrifice if only the favor of God might be restored to me.

While prayer was offered for me, that the Lord would give me strength and courage to bear the message, the thick darkness that had encompassed me rolled back, and a sudden light came upon me. Something that seemed to me like a ball of fire struck me right over the heart. My strength was taken away, and I fell to the floor. I seemed to be in the presence of the angels. One of these holy beings again repeated the words, *"Make known to others what I have revealed to you* [emphasis added]."

Father Pearson, who could not kneel on account of his rheumatism, witnessed this occurrence. When I revived sufficiently to see and hear, he rose from his chair, and said, "I have seen a sight such as I never expected to see. A ball of fire came down from heaven, and struck Sister Ellen Harmon right on the heart. I saw it! I saw it! I can never forget it. It has changed my whole being. Sister Ellen, have courage in the Lord. After this night I will never doubt again. We will help you henceforth, and not discourage you."[122]

Ellen Harmon's reticence to impose her charismatic authority in the face of disbelief had initially made her "sensible that the Spirit of God was grieved." She had been reluctant to pray in public; now she was reluctant to "meet with great opposition" to fulfill the divine command: "Make known to others what I have revealed

122. White, *Life Sketches*, 70. It is more likely than not that Father Pearson did lose faith in Ellen's prophetic status, given the trajectory of the other members of his immediate family.

to you." She had already revealed it to the "little company in Portland, who then fully believed it to be of God." But now she felt she had a "call to travel" more widely. When she did not comply, "the Lord hid his face from me. I was again in darkness and despair." "I was afraid I had grieved the Spirit of the Lord from me forever . . . ."[123] She emphasized her continuity with two previous individuals whom she believed the Lord had called to her same special prophetic, or Messenger, status. According to her recollection of Hazen Foss, his rejection of God's imperative call caused the Spirit of God to be grieved and God departed from him forever, just like He threatened to depart "from me forever."[124] "In my second vision, about a week after the first, the Lord gave me a view of the trials through which I must pass, and told me that I must go and relate to others what He had revealed to me." This second vision elevated her to the stage equivalent to a Methodist itinerant minister. The ecstatic experience which initially had been for her alone was transformed into a community resource that she was obliged to proclaim to others. Ellen Harmon takes great pains to emphasize that the prophetic office was not her idea. Indeed, she vigorously resisted it. But the prophetic call was unrelenting. "[T]he words of the angel sounded continually in my ears, 'Make known to others what I have revealed to you.'" For an indeterminate length of time, (probably less than a month), Ellen was disobedient to the divine imperative. She became extremely depressed but confided in no one. The Little Flock of Portland Millerites "knew that for some reason my mind had become depressed, and they felt that this was sinful on my part, considering the gracious manner in which the Lord had manifested Himself to me."[125]

Then the Disappointed, shut-door Portland Millerites led by Father Pearson ordained her to the Gospel ministry by insisting that she accept God's command to be his special Messenger. Her ecstatic experiences were now *corporately* recognized as God's

123. White, *Spiritual Gifts*, 2:36.
124. Foy had been traditionally assigned to a similar fate. However, recent historians like Baker in *Unknown Prophet* rehabilitated him.
125. White, *Life Sketches*, 69–71.

authoritative new "Word" to the Little Flock. An incipient church entity was conceived at this moment that was the offspring of the Millerite movement but now differentiated itself from it and outlived it. *Ellen Harmon's authority now surpassed that of William Miller's, who was demoted to superseded, if honored elder statesman.* Despite God's special leading in the past, somehow God's Spirit could never persuade Miller of either Ellen Harmon's spiritual authority or of the special status of Saturday Sabbath.

ELLEN'S SLEIGH RIDE TO AVOID J. TURNER'S BRIDEGROOM DOCTRINE

Another critical reason why Ellen Harmon was never able to concede that Miller's date-setting methodology was erroneous, was the fact that she had invested her entire body and soul to its proclamation. All her waking hours were spent in proclaiming the biblically certain fact that the Second Advent would occur on October 22, 1844 and that a terrifying fate was the lot of all who rejected God's last Midnight Cry. This was reinforced by the same prophetic "rolling mountains of flame" announcement proclaimed by William Foy, the "hell, hell, hell" warning of William Miller, and the absolute certainty of S. S. Snow and scores of other Millerite preachers. Ellen was absolutely determined to convert all of her friends and acquaintances—many of them both significantly older and often even married.

> I determined that my efforts *should never cease* till these dear souls, for whom I had so great an interest, yielded to God. *Several entire nights were spent by me in earnest prayer* for those whom I had sought out and brought together for the purpose of laboring and praying with them .... But at every one of our little meetings I continued to exhort and pray for each one separately, until every one had yielded to Jesus, acknowledging the merits of His pardoning love. Every one was converted to God.[126]

---

126. White, *Life Sketches*, 41–42.

After investing such an intense effort in proclaiming the Midnight Cry for October 22, 1844, it was impossible for Ellen Harmon to conceive that God might not be in the "definite time" movement. Additionally, given her endorsement of Foy's "rolling mountains of flame" testimonial in support of October 22, 1844, and given that Foy's predictions were falsified, it is difficult to see how either Foy's or Ellen Harmon's prophetic support for October 22, 1844 can escape the biblical scrutiny of Deut 18:22: "When a prophet speaketh in the name of the LORD, if the thing follow not, nor come to pass, that is the thing which the LORD hath not spoken, but the prophet hath spoken it presumptuously: thou shalt not be afraid of him."

ELLEN HARMON'S FIRST VISION CONFIRMS SNOW'S MIDNIGHT CRY

The central message of Ellen Harmon's First Vision was that the Snow's Midnight Cry was ordained by God. And what was Snow's Midnight Cry? It was that the Second Coming would occur on October 22, 1844. Clearly the earth had not been cleansed by fire as predicted. But *what* had occurred? Ellen Harmon's December 1844 First Vision *did not answer this question*. For the moment, Ellen was content to emphasize that the date-setting of the Midnight Cry was divine light. It was only months later, in January to February 1845, that replacement "comings" to the Second Coming were proposed.

Apollos Hale and Joseph Turner proposed their Bridegroom hypothesis in the Advent Mirror of January 1845. Ellen had her Bridegroom vision *afterwards*. Her Bridegroom vision would mirror Hale's and Turner's Bridegroom explanation for the failure of the Second Coming to occur on October 22, 1844. They asserted that Christ had "come" on October 22, 1844 but only invisibly in the guise of a Bridegroom. Only after his wedding would the Bridegroom "come" visibly to earth as a conquering King. According to the official and authorized editors and annotators of *Ellen G. White, Letters and Manuscripts*, the Bridegroom hypothesis was based on an *allegorical* interpretation of Matt 25's parable of the Bridegroom and the Ten Virgins.

> For Bridegroom Adventists their basic theological argument was drawn from the parable of the ten virgins in Matthew 25. They made the parable *allegorical* to their 1844 experience, and believed that on or about October 22, 1844, Jesus had gone into a heavenly wedding. The *Advent Mirror* divided the marriage into two steps; the actual marriage and the marriage supper.[127]

Then in March 1845, O. R. L. Crosier published a document proposing that the Bridegroom *began* acting as High Priest, for the first time in salvation history, in the Most Holy Place. As High Priest he was now atoning *exclusively* for the sins of Millerites who had accepted the Midnight Cry. In the first stage prior to October 22, 1844, Christ's mediatorial labor was offered to everyone. In the second stage, post-Disappointment, it was available only for the wise virgins inside the shut-door. Before October 22, 1844 Christ had "an important work to do for his enemies with the Father, to make 'intercession for the transgressors,' at the end of which he has a work to do for his saints *exclusively* before their resurrection; then follows his visible Advent . . . ."[128] As Burt notes, Crosier's allegorical "exposition of the earthly and heavenly sanctuaries became a *major foundation* of Seventh-day Adventist theology."[129] It became a major foundation because it was endorsed by Ellen G. White.

In 1847 the newly wedded Ellen G. White became convinced that God showed her that O. R. L. Crosier received "the light" regarding an extended, two-apartment, two-phased, atonement.

> The Lord shew me in vision, more than one year ago, that Brother Crosier had the true light, on the cleansing of the Sanctuary, and that it was his will, that Brother C.

---

127. Burt, "'Shut-door' and Ellen White's Visions," 45.
128. Burt, "Day-Dawn of Canandaigua," 320.
129. Burt, "Day-Dawn of Canandaigua," 317.

should write out the view which he gave us in the *Day-Star, Extra*, February 7, 1846.¹³⁰

Ellen G. White's endorsement of Crosier "true light" virtually ensured the immortality of both his treatment of the "tarrying time" and his conception of an "extended atonement." Her endorsement of Crosier's hypothesis included, of course, his assertion that as of October 22, 1844, Christ as High Priest was atoning "exclusively" for believers in the Midnight Cry. It was the shut-door dogma in another form.

It is highly significant that Ellen Harmon did not offer a verse-by-verse exegesis, like Miller, Snow, Turner, Hale, and Crosier, of the passages that she believed were the biblical basis for the shut-door doctrine. She just promulgates a broad, vague endorsement—without any specifics that can be subject to critical analysis. Rather she simply asserts her visions and prophetic endorsement as sufficient authority for claiming that God had given the "true light" to Crosier and others.

NICHOLS 1851 CHART REPLACES MILLER'S 1843 CHART PER WHITE'S AUTHORITY

Ellen G. White wrote in a June 2, 1853 letter a vision given at Jackson, Michigan:

> I saw that God was in the publishment of the chart by Brother Nichols [Otis Nichols]. I saw that there was a prophecy of this chart in the Bible...."¹³¹

This Nichols chart of 1851 was an updated version of the 1843 Millerite chart that Ellen G. White contended was divinely

---

130. White, "Word To The 'Little Flock,'" 12.

131. White, *Ellen G. White,* 358. The annotator, Karlman, notes that this chart "depicted prophetic symbols from Daniel and Revelation together with time calculations. In October 1850 Ellen White had received instruction in vision that a prophetic chart should be published. During the next few months Otis Nichols supervised the publication of a chart that was advertised for distribution and sale in January 1851."

inspired. In her letters and manuscripts between 1850–1859 there are casual, nonspecific references to "charts" being used as the basis for evangelistic meetings presented by ministers like James White. Most likely these were Otis Nichols's 1850 charts. Turner and Hale's Bridegroom concept and Crosier's "extended atonement" hypothesis were incorporated in this chart into a synthesis of what shortly evolved as the SDA doctrine of the Investigative Judgment.

Ellen Harmon White had reached the pinnacle of her authority when she put her prophetic imprimatur on the "true light" which, she said, God had given to Crosier. In 1851 Ellen G. White personally superintended what became known as the Nichols chart. It portrayed in pictorial format Crosier's thesis expounding a unique cornerstone of SDA theology. It simultaneously cemented *Ellen G. White's power to authoritatively declare who had been given God's divine light.* Ellen G. White *saw* that William Miller had been given divine guidance in arriving at his calculations of the Second Coming. Then Ellen White *saw* that "Brother Crosier had the true light, on the cleansing of the Sanctuary." Finally, Ellen G. White *saw* "God was in the publishment of the chart by Brother Nichols." On October 23, 1850 Ellen White had a vision that simultaneously, retroactively, confirmed the Midnight Cry by affirming that Miller's old 1843 chart was "directed by the Lord." It also affirmed that the new 1851 Nichols chart should closely reflect it and that "not a peg of if should be altered without inspiration." The "inspiration" referred to was *her* inspiration. Thus, the new and improved 1851 chart was the cornerstone foundation for Ellen G. White's theology. This chart has been almost totally forgotten.

> I saw that the truth should be made plain on tables, that the earth and the fullness thereof is the Lord's, and that necessary means should not be spared to make it plain. I saw that the angels' messages, made plain, would have effect. I saw that the old [1843] chart was directed by the Lord, and that not a peg[132] of it should be altered without

---

132. The colloquial equivalent of "not a jot or a tittle."

inspiration.[133] I saw that the figures on the chart were as God wanted them, and that His hand was over and hid a mistake in some of the figures so that none could see it until His hand was removed.[134]

The terrified twelve-year-old Ellen Harmon consumed by the possibility of hell had been transformed into the authoritative Ellen G. White who had been granted the authority to determine who had God's light and that the date-setting Midnight Cry was God's light.

MILLER'S ERRONEOUS THEORIES VS. COMMONSENSE TRUTHS

In my forthcoming book, *Father Miller's Daughter: Ellen Harmon White*, I have documented in detail that both Miller's *method and results* were largely dependent upon disconfirmed sixteenth century Protestant commentators. This is unremarkable except for the fact that Miller conceived of himself as a virtual *tabula rasa*, independent of *any* interpretive tradition—particularly historicism. He was reputedly not dependent on anything except God and his

---

133. As Ellen G. White considered that she was the only person in her epoch who had the gift of inspiration, and as several aspects of the two charts differed, it is clear that Ellen G. White closely supervised the construction of the 1850–51 chart to ensure that "not a peg" of "the figures on the chart" were altered "without [her] inspiration."

134. White, *Ellen G. White*, 242–44. This is the basis of the claim that God deliberately obscured from Miller's view his error in not accounting for the fact that there was no zero year in the transition from BC to AD. This is doubtless the basis for the fact that in Otis Nichols 1850 chart in his lower right corner's "Explanation of the Time," he has equivocated on many of the "exact" prophetic dates. Mrs. White ordered that not a "peg" of the 1843 chart should be modified without her inspiration. Thus, Nichols does not engrave simply 508, 538, or 1798 but rather approximates them as 508–9, 538–9, and 1798–9. This reveals some uncertainty about the exact dates and events that were to have occurred on these dates. Was the "daily" removed in 509, the papacy set up in 539, and did the "time of the end" begin in 1799? Only one date was certain. The 1843 chart was now updated in 1850 to become the October 22, 1844 chart.

concordance. Ellen Harmon reiterated Miller's self-conception. In essence, Miller was not "taught by men" either. Rather, Miller received divine light *de noveau* on Daniel and Revelation via regular angelic guidance. But Miller's and Harmon's paradigm had already been disconfirmed by his predictions about the Ottoman Empire. In *Father Miller's Daughter* I present a detailed case study of the purported collapse of the Ottoman Empire as a contemporaneous case of a falsified historicist prediction—that Harmon, nevertheless, thought had been confirmed. Ellen Harmon's unique psychological and sociological characteristics, her tender age, and the fact that her central nervous system had been shattered, illuminate her susceptibility to Millerism. The out-of-body experiences of Caleb Rich and Richard Randell, their agonizing struggles with the concept of hell's eternal punishment, and the acknowledgement of their prophetic roles by their followers all exhibit parallels to Ellen Harmon's intensely ecstatic experiences—and the response of her and their disciples. The world-famous exploits of Joan of Arc and her claim to direct, divine guidance also parallel Ellen Harmon's self-understanding.

Miller had the self-conception that he was expositing the plain sense or commonsense of scripture. Historians of all stripes have observed that Miller came out of the Scottish Commonsense philosophy with a very rationalist flavor. For example, Jeff Crocombe says: "Above all else, Miller's approach was a rational one."[135] Millerites considered that they had *scientifically, even mathematically*, demonstrated multiple proofs that *the date of the Second Advent could be predicted with precision*. In their literature they also claimed that even their opponents admitted that they could find no errors in their calculations. The claim that their opponents could find no errors is a leitmotif in SDA apologetic literature written ever since. More importantly, this was the perception of Ellen Harmon, aged twelve to sixteen and Ellen White, adult.

This is an enormous irony.

First, a truly "commonsense" interpretation of "no man knoweth the day or hour" could never have allowed Millerites to

---

135. Crocombe, *Feast of Reason*, 72.

not only turn this declaration into its opposite, but to do so with such absolute dogmatism that they branded the "commonsense" warning of Jesus as being terms inspired by evil angels. In short, Miller's critics had accurately identified Millerism's most gargantuan error. Their opposition to his message stiffened precisely when Millerism went over the slippery edge from "about 1843" to "definite time" setting.

Second, opponents did point out other substantial errors on specific major pillars of Miller's fifteen proofs, including proofs that were incorporated into the 1843 chart that Ellen White asserted was endorsed by God. For example, the 1843 chart included a 2520-year interval, from 677 BC to 1843, (Seven Times of the Gentiles), which today not even fundamentalist SDAs attempt to justify. Additionally, "Miller essentially ignored the literary and historical context of a passage and was totally unconcerned with the original author's intent for the original recipients." "Nor was Miller interested in reading the Scriptures in the original languages." Millerism required that the reader disregard the literary and historical context of a passage and disregard the meaning and syntax of the original language. This guarantees that the Bible will be misinterpreted. Thus, George Bush in 1844 pointed out to Miller that his Seven Times of the Gentiles proof, based "mainly upon the reading of the English text of the Scriptures" was plainly in error because "seven times" (even in English) plainly meant that God was threatening Israel that he would punish them with "sevenfold severity" (emphasis in original) and was not an indication of a 2520-year interval of time. Bush concluded that it "cannot be expected that intelligent men will receive any interpretation which is not sustained by the original." Miller blasted Bush with a withering, caustic reply absolutely denying the validity of his points. This was typical Miller. He also blasted other learned exegetes sarcastically on the basis that they were merely using fancy phrases "spotted over with a little Hebrew, Greek, and Latin, all obtained [from] . . . obscure writers, and classical blockheads."[136] Miller regularly expressed an anti-intellectual bias. In short, Millerites imagined

---

136. Crocombe, *Feast of Reason*, 83–84.

themselves as immune from error. They inhabited their own peculiar echo-chamber where they were tone-deaf to any criticism and completely absorbed in their own circular reasoning. Ellen Harmon clearly reflected Miller's anticlerical anti-intellectualism. Ellen White asserted that all who disagreed with Miller were "hypocritical ministers and bold scoffers" who had "united with Satan and his angels."[137]

This made it obvious to young Ellen that all such critics had rejected the light of the Midnight Cry, while God had put his hand over any error that the Millerites *may* have made. But there is no evidence of any kind for Ellen Harmon's meta-narrative other than her own "I saw" assertions. Only if one indulges in circular reasoning and first makes the presumption that Ellen Harmon must be infallible can one assume that her analysis of the Midnight Cry both before 1844 and after December 1844 was correct.

In the immediate post-Disappointment period, both open door, and especially shut-door Adventists were caught up in a maelstrom. Ellen Harmon replaced William Miller, yet she was chronically debilitated and even delirious at times. Miller's convoluted and torturous proofs were quickly lost in the ensuing chaos. Ellen Harmon and the Little Flock had more existentially threatening menaces to surmount. Moreover, Miller's fifteen proofs had been so obviously falsified that no one thought of defending them—or at least fourteen of them.

By promoting his book, the SDA church implicitly ratified F. D. Nichol's evaluation of fourteen of Miller's proofs. Orthodox Seventh-day Adventism tacitly admitted that fourteen proofs were farfetched and fanciful but implied that this made no difference. They made no difference because these fourteen proofs were merely "secondary." They were mere superfluous relics that could be relegated to the dustbin of history. Even the fifteenth proof, Dan 8:14, has experienced a very rocky history even amongst SDA theologians.[138] Thus, the question must be posed: Is it credible that God led Miller to "far-fetched" and "fanciful" expositions of

---

137. White, *Spiritual Gifts*, 1:133–35.
138. Cottrell, "Sanctuary Debate," 16–26.

fourteen of his proofs yet somehow provided an immaculate conception for the fifteenth?

Miller and his Millerites, including Ellen Harmon, did not err solely due to rational, mathematical miscalculations. Harmon erred in her Midnight Cry beliefs because of psychosocial characteristics which predisposed her to millennialist speculations. She and her surrounding circle of eventual disciples developed the symbiotic relationship also displayed in other relationships characteristic of charismatics and their devotees. In Ellen Harmon's case, both she and a small circle of devotees shared certain normative expectations. Physical manifestations displayed by Ellen Harmon and William Foy were irresistible proofs to persons like Father Pearson that these visionaries' messages were divinely inspired. These bodily proofs were just as convincing as Miller's fifteen mathematico-biblical proofs. Bernadette Soubirous is another classical case of how such psychosocial dynamics operate.

BERNADETTE SOUBIROUS AND LOURDES: PSYCHO-SOCIAL MILIEU LIKE EGW'S

There are significant religio-psycho-social-economic parallels between Ellen Harmon and Bernadette Soubirous. The Bernadette Soubirous of international Lourdes fame falls intermediate in social antecedents between Ellen Harmon and Caleb Rich and Richard Randel. Whereas Caleb Rich, Universalist Visionary, Richard Randel, Freewill Baptist, and Ellen Harmon were all staunch Protestants, Bernadette Soubirous and Ellen Harmon shared their femininity. This alone made them unlikely candidates to head a religious movement.

Bernadette Soubirous was born the year of the Great Disappointment in 1844. She entered the world's stage on February 11, 1858 when at age fourteen she reported the first of eighteen Marian apparitions in Lourdes, France. When Ellen Harmon was fourteen, she had just experienced Miller's second preaching tour to Portland, Maine, followed by an ecstatic experience of baptism into the Methodist church and Millerite Message. Whereas Ellen

Harmon's success can be measured in the twenty million Seventh-day Adventists recorded as members, the success Bernadette Soubirous achieved can be measured in the five million pilgrims attracted annually to the healing waters of Lourdes. Ellen Harmon and Bernadette Soubirous share other social characteristics. Ellen Harmon's First Vision occurred in an exclusively feminine social support system. Just a handful of women had met at Elizabeth Haines's house for prayer. Similarly, Bernadette's ecstatic first experience was witnessed solely by two young, female playmates. On February 14, 1858, during the second apparition only about a dozen young girls returned to where the Marian apparition had first appeared. The next several apparitions were also witnessed solely by women. It was not until the sixth apparition that men deigned to pay any attention to what they considered a mere childhood prank. Police Commissioner Dominique Jacomet brought Bernadette in for questioning on February 21, 1858 after the sixth apparition. He threatened her with prison if she went back anywhere near the grotto where the apparition had initially appeared. The imperial prosecutor, Vital Dutour, attempted to scare Bernadette into a recantation. Yet, Jean-Baptiste Estrade, the local tax collector, became "instantly convinced that Bernadette was genuine." He said that Bernadette was like "an angel of prayer, reflecting in her face all the raptures of heaven."[139]

Bernadette's socioeconomic circumstances paralleled Ellen's in other ways. Bernadette's and Ellen's youth made them suspect in the judgment of the local patriarchy. Ellen records specifically that many of those doubting her spiritual gift considered that God would more likely chose an older, wiser, and male person for his

---

139. Harris, *Lourdes*, 63. See also page 194 for the tale of Pere Cros who, meeting Bernadette for the first time in 1864 became utterly convinced of the verity of her experience. "It was Bernadette herself who swept away the doubts of a man highly cautious about miracle tales." This mirrors Joseph Bates attitude toward Ellen Harmon. He was initially very cautious and hesitant to credit Ellen Harmon's claims. He closely interrogated her closest associates searching for alternate explanations. It was only an astronomy vision which convinced him, making him the happiest man he could imagine. Father Cros functioned in just such a role in respect to Bernadette Soubirous.

messenger. Bernadette was treated with great skepticism by the all-male local dignitaries. Both Ellen and Bernadette displayed a stubborn charisma that eventually broke through the initial resistance of the local patriarchy.

Another determinative social feature that Ellen and Bernadette shared was their very ill health. Ellen's traumatic brain injury when she was nine apparently resulted in lifelong, chronic illness. She self-reports that she is chronically, repeatedly, almost at death's door. Repeatedly, when she has a sympathetic audience before her hanging on every oracular word, she is miraculously revived. It is as if she requires an audience to pray her back to health so that she can relate her visions. Similarly, Bernadette's family was so poor that she was chronically malnourished and sickly. Their father was arrested for stealing a bag of wheat from his employer. They were functionally homeless, being reduced to lodging in an old, dilapidated Lourdes prison. Only three years previously, in 1855 Bernadette suffered from cholera. (As did the extended James and Ellen White household in the 1850s as well.) Furthermore, she likely had already contracted the tuberculosis that killed her in 1879 in her mid-thirties. (James White's young brother and sister also died of tuberculosis in his own lodgings). Ellen Harmon was, of course, characterized by her supporters as the weakest of the weak. Their spiritual strength and physical afflictions were shared characteristics.

Despite the initial skepticism exhibited by local male officials, the regional religious context was favorable for both Bernadette and Ellen. Ellen's rise to spiritual authority was benefitted from the fact that the dominant New England culture was Protestant, anti-Catholic, and had a notable penchant towards apocalyptic millennialism. The basic tenets of Millerism were already inscribed in the footnotes printed in her 1822 KJV Family Bible and there was a widespread belief amongst her neighbors that signs like the *aurora borealis*, an 1833 meteorite shower, and a 1780 Dark Day all presaged an imminent end of the world. Conversely, Bernadette's message was equally well adapted to the ambient, dominant Catholic worldview where Marian apparitions were widespread and anticipated with an expectancy similar to Ellen's expected millennium.

There were forty Marian shrines within a radius of twenty five kilometers from Lourdes. Several miraculous apparitions of the Virgin Mary had recently occurred. In 1830 the Virgin Mary had purportedly appeared to a Catherine Laboure resulting in the minting of a medallion of this miracle which sold in the millions. The Virgin Mary also appeared in 1842 to a Jewish Alsatian named Alphonse Ratisbonne, resulting in a well-publicized conversion. In 1846 Mary had appeared to shepherd children at La Salette, a nearby hamlet, causing a storm of publicity. Additionally, local legends had it that cultic statues of Notre-Dame escaped captivity, traversed mountain slides, and swam across rivers in order to return to their preferred cultic sites. In short, the peasants of Lourdes were perfectly primed to expect apparitions. It was not just the peasants. The local priest, Peyramale, shared their superstitious bent. He recounted to his brother the tale that he had been escorted through the woods by a pack of gentle wolves, sent by providence to protect him on a dark, cold, snowy night.

The global religious environment was auspicious. France was the central battleground for a showdown between secular, Republican forces represented by Voltaire, the philosophes, and Emile Zola, and hierarchical, monarchical, clerical forces represented by an ultramontane papacy. Catholic France was ripe for a miraculous, iconic symbol around which pietistic Catholics could rally. Just four years prior, in 1854, Pope Pius IX had proclaimed the dogma of the Immaculate Conception, the belief that not only was Mary an eternal Virgin and Theotokos (Bearer of God), but she had also miraculously been spared the curse of Original Sin. Late in the series of apparitions when the local crowds, now numbering in the thousands, had repeatedly demanded the official identity of the apparition, Bernadette reported that the apparition had said: "*Que soy era Immaculada Councepciou*" or "I am the Immaculate Conception." Nothing could more perfectly fit the well-honed preconceptions of both the papal curia at the Vatican and the local populace.

Moreover, like Ellen's miraculous bodily signs during vision, Bernadette's authenticity was also attested by miraculous occurrences. Bernadette's highly unusual behavior had already convinced her audience that these manifestations had to be either from God or from the devil. She was repeatedly and vigorously tested for indications of pious fraud which she passed with flying colors. She declined to profit personally from her "gift" and refused favors including everything down to the proverbial crust of bread. She remained steadfastly humble even when repeatedly humiliated by ecclesiological and civic authorities. Even Protestants were impressed by her saintly behavior: "Few contemporaries, even those who refused to believe her, ever doubted her sincerity."[140] Thus, the consensus of the masses was that her gift was divine and not demonic. Thousands of observers witnessed that Bernadette's face shone with a luminous, divine, translucent light. Her hand remained in the direct flame of a candle but, like Daniel and the three worthies, came out unscathed. Another skeptic gave her a trial by ordeal, plunging a "big pin with a black head" into Bernadette's shoulder without eliciting any response. Today, these minor miracles are all overshadowed by more stupendous claims. Instantaneous and permanent cures of incurable, fatal diseases, confirmed by rigorous medical examinations of both the healed and their medical records are now claimed. Ellen's supporters reported that physicians confirmed her breathlessness. Those who heard her speak noted that her chronically ill lungs and upper airways seemed to spontaneously heal during her visions or when she was relating them. Bernadette's supporters obtained the testimony of three physicians who certified the supernatural nature of Bernadette's experience.

> In the presence of the apparition, she was even momentarily cured of her illnesses: As soon as the Blessed Virgin appeared to Bernadette, her coughing stopped, her breath seemed to die away; her lungs which, a moment

---

140. Harris, *Lourdes*, 51.

before, had breathed the air so laboriously, now seemed no longer to need it.[141]

Ellen Harmon reported that the bright light of heaven during her visions seemed to blind her and that she had difficulty adjusting to the darkness below. Similarly, when Bernadette awoke from her ecstatic encounters, she had to "rub her eyes to adjust them to the relative darkness after the glowing light of the apparition."[142]

In short, if one had observed Bernadette Soubirous in 1857, one would have hardly predicted that she was a likely candidate to create the world-famous, religious, healing center at Lourdes France. Similarly, if one had observed Ellen Harmon in the 1840s, one would have hardly predicted that she would spearhead a religious movement claiming adherents of twenty million parishioners in 2021. Both were pubescent, chronically ill, poorly educated, impoverished, rustic females, a combination of factors which made them both imminently unlikely candidates to spearhead worldwide religious revivals.

A central and crucial similarity to the trajectory of Ellen Harmon and Bernadette Soubirous is their perfectly symbiotic fit with their respective socio-religious milieu. No visionary can take root and found a religious movement without being recognized by a core group of believers. The visionaries themselves, of course, must have a personal charisma, a forceful personality, and a persistent vision that insistently attempts to propagate itself. However, equally critical is their symbiotic relationship to their first disciples. A prophet or prophetess who is never recognized by his own contemporaries, never becomes a prophet.

JOAN OF ARC'S SIMILARITIES WITH ELLEN HARMON

In addition to Bernadette Soubirous, William Foy, Richard Randel, and Caleb Rich, Joan of Arc's mission and passion shows

---

141. Harris, *Lourdes*, 65.
142. Harris, *Lourdes*, 64.

remarkable similarities to Ellen Harmon's. Joan's statements, like Ellen Harmon's revealed an absolute conviction that she had been irresistibly commanded by God to be his messenger. Both felt compelled to deliver their message. Both were successful in convincing their initial followers that they had been sent by God.

The most obvious similarity between Joan of Arc and Ellen Harmon is their sex and age. This is particularly striking because young female prophetesses run against type. Females faced strong biblical prejudices against filling roles of religious authority. An additional factor is that both were either virtually illiterate or had almost no theological education. Yet their self-defined divine calling shattered all societal barriers.

Both became absolutely convinced that God was speaking and, more importantly, acting through them. Ellen Harmon received her divine communications via ecstatic visions that prostrated her. Joan of Arc received her divine communications via saints. Had Ellen Harmon claimed saints as her source, her Protestant milieu would have never accepted her prophetic gift. Had Joan of Arc received hers via prostrating visions which contained a millennialist message, the most Catholic King and court of Europe would never have accepted her gift. That is to say that despite transgressing certain cultural expectations, they fit other presuppositions of their subculture.

Second, they succeeded in convincing a key constituency that God was acting through them. Why? Because they delivered miraculous omens that meshed with the demands required of them. It was in the French Monarchy's interest to believe that God had sent the Maid, even if she was young and female. Joan performed miraculous feats of arms that benefitted the French Monarch. The Protestants of Ellen Harmon's time could quote Scripture saying that even female slaves (KJV: maid servants) would be blessed with the Holy Spirit. It was in the interest of the Disappointeds to be reassured that their hope in an imminent Second Advent was still imminent. They had not been wrong that God was "in" the Midnight Cry. Indeed, this was *the* crux of Ellen Harmon's First Vision.

The following brief resume of Joan of Arc's life and death illuminate in more concrete and persuasive colors the abstract analysis above.

> "Very illustrious Lord Dauphin, I am come, being sent on the part of God, to give succour to the kingdom and to you." Joan of Arc's first words to Charles VII

> "You men of England, who have no right in this kingdom of France, the king of heaven orders and commands you through me, Joan the Maid, to abandon your strongholds and go back to your own country. If not, I will make a war-cry that will be remembered forever." Joan of Arc to the English at Orleans, May 5, 1429

Joan unreservedly and categorically claimed that God spoke through her as directly as to any other prophet in history. She was just as categorical with Charles VII of France, the Dauphin, as she was uncompromising with the English. She predicted that God had anointed her with the double mission to first lift the English siege of Orleans and then conduct the Dauphin to his solemn consecration as King of France at Reims.

> There are 'two reasons for which I have been sent by the King of Heaven,' Joan said. 'One is to raise the siege of Orleans, the other to lead the King to Reims for his anointing and coronation.[143]

Marvelously, millions of Catholics would say miraculously, both her prophecies were fulfilled in only days whereas the siege had already been dragging on for six months and the English had been chastising the French in the Hundred Years War (1337–1453) for decades. Moreover, the Dauphin's forces had just suffered a devastating defeat trying to lift the siege of Orleans.

Joan entertained no doubts about the divine origin of her mission. She was born in 1412. Only three years later at the Battle of Agincourt, (October 25, 1415), the English had slaughtered the French. When God first spoke to Joan in 1425, she was a mere thirteen-year-old, devout prepubescent. Henry V, the English

---

143. Harrison, *Joan of Arc*, 88.

Child of the Apocalypse

monarch, claimed he was the rightful king of France and had allied himself with the French Duke of Burgundy, transforming the invasion into a devastating civil war. Together they controlled the northern half of France, including Paris. Joan's natal hamlet was in the middle of no-man's land. Midday in the summer of her thirteenth year while church bells chimed, Joan received " a voice from God to help and guide me." Jean Waterin, a childhood friend, later testified that Jean typically "used to go down on her knees every time she heard the bell tolled" when she would slip away to "speak with God." Suddenly, her earthly surroundings vanished, there was nothing but light, "a great deal of light on all sides, as was most fitting," Joan later explained. The voice said, "Be good, go to church often." "It was St. Michael, Joan said, "and he was not alone, but accompanied by many angels from heaven, a great host of angels. St. Gabriel was among them."[144] This was not seeing metaphorically. When the examiners who eventually determined to burn her at the stake demanded: "Did you see St. Michael and these angels corporeally and in reality?" Joan unequivocally replied: "I saw them with my bodily eyes as well as I see you." Like Christ, Joan warned her persecutors: "If you were well informed about me, you would wish me to be out of your hands. *I have done nothing except by revelation*" [emphasis added]. Like Christ, living in obscurity after his presentation in the Temple at age twelve, Joan had kept her encounters with God's voice a secret for several years. Meanwhile, like Enoch, she lived a life apart from other girls who, like her friend Mengette, observed that she was "too pious." In place of earthly companions, she communed with God in the woods, where "I easily heard the voices come to me." By the spring of 1428 the voices told her to present herself to Sir Robert de Baudricourt who was commissioned by God to give her an escort to the Dauphin Charles. Joan explained to Durand Laxart, Joan's mother's cousin's husband, that he was to accompany her to Sir Robert de Baudricourt because "I was to go to the Dauphin, to have him crowned." On May 13, 1428, Laxart brought her to Baudricourt. Baudricourt thought the idea preposterous if not scandalous and suggested that Laxart "give her

---

144. Castor, *Joan of Arc*, 34–35.

a good slapping and take her back to her father." On October 12, 1428 the Dauphin's position declined disastrously when his rivals laid siege to Orleans. If it fell, the Dauphin concluded that his claim to the throne would go extinct and/or he would have to exile himself abroad. In December 1428, Joan took radical measures and left her village to again importune Baudricourt at Vaucouleurs. She was claiming to be the virgin of ancient prophecies who would deliver France *in extremis*. When a doubtful squire, Jean de Metz, gloomily reproached her saying: "Is it not fated that the King (Charles VII) shall be driven from his kingdom, and that we shall all turn English?" She stoutly replied that God had ordained the salvation of France through her—"for that she was born."[145] Although some of the unwashed masses appeared to have begun to put their faith in her at this point, none of the educated aristocracy was yet converted. As Seguin, dean of the faculty of Poitiers, would later tell her at her probationary trial there: "God cannot wish us to believe in you unless he sends us a sign, to show that we should believe in you. We cannot advise the King to entrust you with soldiers, whom you would run into danger, merely on your bare assertion. Have you nothing more to say?"[146]

Academics give a label to the process and method of determining how and on what basis a human mind comes to reliably "know" something: epistemology. *But how can any mind know whether or not God is speaking through the intermediary of another human mind?* (Be that mind Ellen Harmon's or Joan of Arc's?) In this case, the pivotal question is: Is Joan's voice the voice of God? If so, *how* does one know? Paradoxically, even more fascinating is the question: Did Joan genuinely believe that her voice was the voice of God? Or was she merely a highly motivated and skilled motivational speaker? Her seventh trial would conclusively demonstrate that she was willing to die to substantiate her assertion to be the voice of God. Should that be enough to prove her sincerity? Even assuming the answer to this question is yes, is that enough to prove

---

145. Harrison, *Joan of Arc*, 62.
146. Harrison, *Joan of Arc*, 104.

that her voice really was the voice of God? Or was she merely one of the most sincerely mistaken personages of all history?

The theological professors at Poitiers were proposing that Joan demonstrate a sign from God to prove her authenticity. Her rebuke recalled Jesus' rebuke to the Sanhedrin: "I have not come to Poitier to make signs. But lead me to Orleans, and I will show you the signs I was sent to make."[147] The strength of evidence Joan was required to demonstrate was remarkably high. What she was demanding them to believe was diametrically opposed to every truth they had been inculcated with since childhood, prejudices rooted in centuries of Christian misogyny. Regardless of whether her interrogators where English or French, the unanimous opinion of the age was:

> If she had truly been sent by God, she would not wear men's clothes in contravention of God's law and the Church's teaching. The nature of her supposed mission was no excuse for this abomination, since no "greater" good could ever justify sin—and in any case women were forbidden to fight, just as they were forbidden to preach, to teach, to administer the sacraments, and all other duties that belonged [exclusively] to men.[148]

King Henry of England issued an edict January 3, 1431 that was even more blunt:

> It is sufficiently notorious and well known how for some time, a woman who calls herself Joan the Maid has put off the habit and dress of the female sex, which is contrary to divine law, abominable to God, condemned and prohibited by every law; she has dressed and armed herself in the habit and role of a man, has committed and carried out cruel murders and, it is said, has led the simple people to believe, through seduction and deceit, that she was sent from God, and that she had knowledge of His divine secrets, together with several other very

---

147. Harrison, *Joan of Arc*, 104.
148. Castor, *Joan of Arc*, 144.

dangerous dogmas, most prejudicial and scandalous to our holy catholic faith.[149]

Whether viewed from the standpoint of the prejudices of either friend or foe, Joan's quest was the social and spiritual equivalent of scaling a Mount Everest. Yet, Joan's supreme confidence in the divinity of her mission is demonstrated by the preemptory letter she sent the King of England and his court:

> Restore to the Maid, *who is sent here by God*, the king of heaven, the keys of all the fine towns that you have taken and violated in France.
>
> King of England, if you do not do this, I am the military leader, and wherever I find your men in France, I will make them leave, whether they want to or not, and if they will not obey, I will have them all killed. *I am sent here by God, the king of heaven*, to face you head to head and drive you out of the whole of France . . . . for you will never hold the kingdom of France from God, the king of heaven, holy Mary's son; but King Charles will hold it, the true heir, *because God, the king of heaven, wishes it, and this is revealed to him by the Maid* [emphasis added] . . . .[150]

Joan repeatedly asserted complete confidence in her divine credentials in the face of the most entrenched prejudice and opposition imaginable. Her fixed conviction that she was God's voice is undeniable. And unless she had a perverse obsession with martyrdom combined with a psychopathic genius at prevarication, it would be incredible to consider her belief in her voices conscious fakery. Confabulation is a more likely explanation.

But if Joan was irremediably convicted that God spoke through her, were the French masses and the French court also sincerely convinced? Or were they merely making a cynical calculation?

The French court, particularly Yolande, the Dauphin's mother-in-law, was favorably predisposed to female visionaries. Besides

---

149. Castor, *Joan of Arc*, 164.
150. Castor, *Joan of Arc*, 98.

the Hundred Year War, the civil war between the Burgundian factions and the Armagnac factions of French royalty, France had also recently had to endure the Black Death, and civil war within the Catholic Church. Joan was born during the Great Western Schism, the period from 1378 to 1417, when there were two, and later three, rival popes, each with his own following, his own Sacred College of Cardinals, mutually denouncing each other as the antichrist. It was a time that called forth apocalyptic visionaries.

In 1388 a Marie Robine suffering from an incurable illness was miraculously healed at Avignon, administrative seat of one of the rival popes. On February 22, 1398 this holy recluse received a voice from heaven ordering her to command the king to reform the church and end the schism. It was this corruption that caused God to chastise France by means of the devilish English invaders. The Dauphin's mother-in-law, Yolande, was familiar with Marie Robine's revelations. Jeanne-Marie de Maille, a noble lady, also had visions and prophecies about the schism. She had audiences with Charles VI (probably insane from schizophrenia), and spent time with Yolande. Yolande was a witness for Marie Robine at the canonization hearings considering her for sainthood.

Thus, the mother-in-law of the man who Joan wished to make king put credence in female visionaries, predecessors of Joan. When Yolande heard about Joan's stymied attempts to reach the court, she made arrangements for Joan to be received with more enthusiasm. Georges de la Trémoïlle, Charles VII's ruthless favorite, had destroyed Joan's letter to the Dauphin and continued to do his utmost to undermine Joan's growing influence. Jean Gerson, the eminence grise of French theologians, whilst not personally hostile, had written formal theological treatises on "The Discernment of Spirits" to judge just such cases. According to the Holy Scriptures, women in general, he wrote, were "excessive, over eager, changeable, unbridled, and therefore not to be trusted."[151] "Satan's deceptions were practiced more easily on women, whose moral and intellectual frailties made them more susceptible than men to demonic influence." Joan appeared to be the classic text-book case

---

151. Castor, *Joan of Arc*, 91.

of all these vices. Thus, Charles VII faced an insoluble dilemma. God was already punishing France for its iniquities. If the most Christian monarch ordered his flock to follow a false prophetess, a roguish tool of the devil in the guise of a woman, France might be sinning irremediably. On the other hand, if the Dauphin rejected the divine counsel of a true prophet, inspired by the king of heaven, he might be committing the unpardonable sin. Thus, after multiple formal physical determinations that her virginity was intact, Joan faced a rigorous interrogation by eighteen of the most eminent theologians of France, chaired by Regnault de Chartres, archbishop of Reims. Joan's case was unprecedented. Other well-chaperoned female visionaries had communicated divine revelations; but Joan, wearing the abomination of men's clothes and surrounded by bawdy soldiers, was proposing to lead the king's army into battle. Like the test of Gideon's fleece, the convocation determined that should Joan actually lift the siege of Orleans this would be the miraculous sign they sought. On the other hand, showing Solomonic discretion, "to doubt or discard her without there being any appearance of evil in her, would be to reject the Holy Spirit and render oneself unworthy of God's help."[152] Besides, there were two prophecies which applied to Joan. A chronogram attributed to the Venerable Bede pictured a maid bearing a banner, just like Joan. The sage, Merlin, prophesied: "A virgin ascends the backs of the archers, and hides the flower of her virginity," surely a veiled reference to Joan. Moreover, Joan displayed divine foreknowledge. The Dauphin disguised himself as a commoner in a crowd of courtiers and a doppelgänger impersonated the king when Joan was to be introduced to the monarch for the first time. Joan immediately recognized the king despite the ruse.[153] She also successfully predicted that she would locate a mystical sword inside a coffer at the high altar of the church at Sainte-Catherine-de

---

152. Castor, *Joan of Arc*, 96–97.

153. Like Joseph Bates's famous Astronomy Vision, some of these portents may be unreliably attested; however, the unbridled enthusiasm of the mass of both knights and peasants demonstrated their genuine, if possibly unjustified, faith in Joan's voices.

Fierbois that had not been opened for twenty years, her own Excalibur.[154] Joan also foretold the untimely death of a man who mocked her at Chinon, France.[155] The brute fact that Joan's small band had crossed 350 miles of hostile territory to arrive before the Dauphin at Chinon was already a minor miracle. Thus, when Joan successfully lifted the siege of Orleans in only four days, despite his misgivings about the female sex, the skeptical Gerson was forced to conclude: "This deed was done by God."[156]

After God's deed at Orleans, Joan triumphantly led the king on a victory tour through Troyes, Chalons, and other towns on the approaches to Reims where on July 11, 1429 the Dauphin received the divine oil at the Reims Cathedral—with Joan proclaiming: "Noble king, God's will is done."

Thus, despite the fact that Joan's acts and essence shattered all previous precedent, the historical facts were now indubitably established. God had sanctioned her mission with unmistakable tokens of divine favor. The assortment of miracles and portents that accompanied Joan's mission certainly rivaled the physical signs attached to Ellen Harmon's career, be they being prostrated in breathless ecstasy (like Foy) or holding up weighty Bibles while pointing out texts. The three rival popes of the Great Western Schism had names that would soon be forgotten, but Joan of Arc's renown would be immortal. Meanwhile, her acts of exceptional valor on the field and the sacrificial deaths of numerous French warriors would prove beyond a doubt that they all believed that God's voice in Joan's voice had once again decided who ruled France by the divine right of kings.

Another indication of her sincerity is that despite becoming gravely ill, being denied Holy Communion, and being threatened with torture unless she abjured her claims that her pronouncements had the authority of divine revelation, she would not retract. On May 24, 1431, threatened with imminent death, she signed a prepared abjuration which she shortly thereafter revoked stating

---

154. Castor, *Joan of Arc*, 99–100.
155. Harrison, *Joan of Arc*, 86–87.
156. Castor, *Joan of Arc*, 113.

that her voices had censured her with treason for having signed the abjuration. She was then burnt alive. While being burnt she maintained that her voices were sent of God and had not deceived her.

> If I were condemned and saw the fire and the faggots alight and the executioner ready to kindle the fire, and even if I myself were in it, I would say nothing else. I would maintain until death what I said in the trial.[157]

CONCLUSION

Many of Ellen Harmon's critics have questioned her sincerity and honesty.[158] Even more have doubted the honesty of the SDA church's depiction of Ellen Harmon. Certainly, early SDA historians like John Loughborough have been found to have embellished accounts of marvelous happenings.[159] Ellen Harmon herself gave supernatural explanations to events surrounding Israel Dammon whereas disinterested law authorities only noted mass resistance by Dammon's colleagues.[160] However, this manuscript supports another hypothesis. Namely, that a twelve-year-old girl whose nervous system had been shattered was subjected to "scientific" and "exact" Millerism with apparently overwhelming scriptural and mathematical proofs that the Second Coming would occur on October 22, 1844. Furthermore, as an analysis of several religious seers has demonstrated, such persons with intense experiences with the *mysterium tremendum* can be sincerely convinced that their experiences are the result of direct revelation and a divine commission. In any case, as several of Ellen Harmon's cherished predictions failed, she and those who persisted in the movement became radicalized and psychosocially isolated. This exposed

157. Harrison, *Joan of Arc*, 289.
158. Daily, *Ellen G. White: A Psychobiography* is one of the most recent examples.
159. For example, see Strayer, *J. N. Loughborough*.
160. Hoyt, "Trial of Elder I. Dammon," 29–36.

them to small group-think dynamics. Millerites became extremely resistant to any facts or arguments which disconfirmed their initial beliefs because these came from outsiders who they considered to be unbelieving scoffers. Snow's categorical rejection of mainline Christianity's teaching that no man could know the day or hour is the quintessential expression of Millerite dogmatism. Especially when he said: "If they hear not MOSES and the PROPHETS, neither will they be persuaded, although one arose from the dead." Meanwhile, the rapidly shrinking "Little Flock" became exquisitely attuned to the echo-chamber phenomenon. Ellen was only able to accept "facts" and information which reinforced her belief in the date-setting Midnight Cry. It is no reflection on her sincerity that she was too immature, uneducated, and sociologically isolated to discern that the date-setting inherent in allegorical-typological-historicism had been disconfirmed multiple times by failed predictions. Promoters of enthusiastic millennialism through the centuries generally did not lack in sincerity; they lacked in spiritual discernment. In conformity with this pattern, Ellen Harmon was unable to accurately discern the impossible allegorical interpretations that S. S. Snow imposed upon biblical texts from Jeremiah, Ezekiel, and Habakkuk, texts which were the *quintessential foundation* of his date-setting Midnight Cry. She became both convinced and converted by Snow's Midnight Cry. Given the fact that she was only twelve to sixteen years of age during the zenith of Millerism, she really cannot be expected to have had the mental capacity to judge the validity and accuracy of Miller's and Snow's fifteen proofs. What she relied on existentially was her intensely personal experience of ecstasy and the dreams and visions of a beautiful, merciful Jesus who assured her of salvation *through Millerite date-setting*. Methodism's theologically abstruse concepts of justification and sanctification were insufficiently concrete and physical to give her assurance. Until her personal encounters with Miller and William Foy, she was convinced that she was destined for hell. She was convinced that if she abandoned the Midnight Cry, she would be bound for hell, as Miller proclaimed. Thus, it was psychologically impossible for her to consider the possibility that the October 22, 1844 date might be wrong.

Despite overwhelming evidence that disconfirmed August 11, 1840, March 21, 1844, and October 22, 1844, Miller's *multiple*, definite dates for the Second Coming, her mind was blocked to this reality. After Snow's Midnight Cry assertion that the Second Coming would occur on October 22, 1844, she was totally convinced that Christ would come on this date and she would become immortal. The failure of this prediction did not dissuade her from Miller's allegorical-typological-historicism. She remained captive to its appeal. *After* Apollos Hale and Joseph Turner used this *same* methodology to arrive at their Bridegroom hypothesis, she ratified their conclusion in her own Bridegroom vision. When O. R. L. Crosier continued to apply the allegorical-typological-historicist methodology, she was predisposed to accept the Crosier hypothesis of an extended atonement, claiming that God had given Crosier the "true light." As a consequence, although Ellen Harmon White continued to have vision after vision that proclaimed that the Second Coming was only months or, at most, a year or two distant, Crosier's extended atonement has lasted from 1844 to 2021. Despite these failures of prophecy, the SDA church has been locked into promulgating an entire multifaceted assortment of Miller's original celestial signs and "exact" prophetic intervals. Not on the original, purportedly biblical basis that Miller, Snow or Crosier *actually* gave—but existentially, because of what a twelve-year-old listening to William Miller heard in 1840, as confirmed by what the same sixteen-year-old heard listening to William Foy in March 1844 and Snow in August 1844.

There is an *unbroken causal link* between William Miller's 1840 influence on the twelve-year-old Ellen Harmon, William Foy's March 1844 influence on sixteen-year-old Ellen Harmon, and S. S. Snow's, Joseph Turner's, and O. R. L. Crosier's influence on Ellen Harmon during the 1844–1846 interval. What they all had in common was their use of the allegorical-typological-historicist "method" in explaining eschatological biblical passages. They were convinced that it was guaranteed to predict the date for the

Second Coming because they thought it was simultaneously scientific, mathematical, biblical, objective, literal, and supported by commonsense. However, in actual practice, it was *fanciful, allegorical, capricious,* and the *opposite* of a plain, commonsense, literal reading of the text. When Christ said no man would know the day or hour of the Second Coming, it was not commonsense or literal to preach the opposite. Yet that is precisely what occurred. William Miller, S. S. Snow, and Ellen Harmon convinced themselves that their allegorical interpretations were literal, but any reader examining their *original* expositions can confirm that this is not the case. Her ecstatic experience, which she equated with *immediate revelation,* not the literal text, was the second decisive element in determining Ellen Harmon's doctrinal conclusions. She and her followers came to the conclusion that her visions were direct revelations from the divine Mind. In a formal statement at an 1855 conference her supporters adopted the resolution that we "hold these views [her visions] as emanating from the divine Mind."[161]

The clearest evidence of the primacy of ecstatic, immediate revelation compared to the lesser influence of the biblical text are the stories that Ellen herself relates in regards to her own doubts about her prophetic gifts. One highly significant anecdote was her tale of the fifty golden texts that she says were shown to her when she claims to have been struck dumb—as a consequence of doubt. She *never* provided a verse-by-verse, word-by-word grammatical, syntactical exposition of any of Miller's theories.[162] Rather, she regularly cites the fact that her supporters and herself have been

161. Levterov, *Development,* 73.

162. Ellen Harmon does not provide verse-by-verse contextual exegesis. Rather she simply asserts a general endorsement to the allegorical-historicist expositions of others, specifically Miller, Snow and Crosier, saying they have the "true light." No SDA expositor has actually ever demonstrated that any of these men's writings contain a defensible, literal, commonsense justification of their theses. To the contrary, SDA apologists like F. Nichol and Merlin Burt concede that these men's expositions are *farfetched, fanciful, and allegorical.* Yet, because Ellen Harmon claimed that these men's expositions contained the "true light," and that Miller came to his conclusions based on divine guidance, these men's farfetched and allegorical expositions remain the cornerstone foundation of unique SDA dogmas.

prostrated by what they presumed must be the Holy Ghost. She emphasizes that even her detractors have been prostrated. Father Pearson and the Pearson brothers were persuaded to support both William Foy and Ellen Harmon due to the extraordinary physical phenomena they displayed. In the case of the anecdote of selective psychogenic mutism and the fifty golden verses, Ellen Harmon does her best to convince her audience that a supernatural event has confirmed her prophetic authenticity and authority. When the Jews demanded signs from Jesus, it is said that he refused. Ellen Harmon, in contrast, repeatedly, although implicitly, argued that various paranormal signs proved her prophetic credentials. Arthur White, her grandson, would still appeal to such paranormal events to buttress her prophetic credentials in his biography.[163]

Ellen Harmon, was subject to the same laws of religious enthusiasm that have determined the conclusions of those who become persuaded that they had been favored with immediate revelation. As Lovejoy noted, religious enthusiasts in the New World "all boasted an intimacy with God, who spoke *directly* to them." Therefore, they concluded that their dogmas and social movements "formed the *unquestionable* truth behind their inspiration [emphasis added]." Debatable, theological *abstractions* like justification, sanctification were far less psychologically satisfying than ecstatic, direct, and b*odily* revelations. Lovejoy cites Anne Hutchinson as one example of this psychological dynamic. The bodily certainty of prostration gave both Hutchinson and Millerites a self-assured, uncompromising stridency that condemned an erudite, scoffing clergy as Babylon. Hutchinson concluded that "'no sanctification can help to evidence to us our justification.' The 'ground of all was assurance by immediate revelation* [emphasis added]." On the same basis, Ellen Harmon was fully persuaded that her immediate revelation, in conjunction with Miller's fifteen biblical-mathematical proofs, gave her a perfect assurance that she could find nowhere else. Lovejoy further illustrates this phenomenon as he describes the "prophet Hendrik Niclaes who set himself up in Holland about 1540 in answer to a divine command to

---

163. White, *Ellen G. White*, 275.

establish a new sect." Like Ellen Harmon and Caleb Rich, Niclaes claimed that "he owed nothing to men's ministry but only to the mouth of God, whose voice he heard."[164] Ellen's claim that "It Was Not Taught Me by Man" was her version of the stock disclaimer issued by multiple visionaries.[165]

Like Joan of Arc, Bernadette Soubirous, William Foy, Caleb Rich, and Richard Randel, Ellen Harmon was fully persuaded that she had had ecstatic, out-of-body experiences culminating in a *direct, unmediated experience of the divine.*[166] This direct revelation substantiated the message of the Midnight Cry. As a result, the crucial burden of her First Vision was that what she "saw" proved the validity and veracity of the Midnight Cry despite all historical and biblical proof to the contrary. By historical, I refer to the fact that Snow's prediction of October 22, 1844 was historically falsified. By biblical, I refer to the fact that Miller's and Snow's interpretation of their numerous biblical texts was plainly farfetched and fanciful. Nevertheless, Ellen Harmon and her disciples were persuaded that her paranormal, bodily manifestations proved that she had been endowed by the Holy Spirit with the gift of prophecy.[167] Thus, when she "saw" that God had given William Miller divine light on the prophecies, when she "saw" that God was "in" the Midnight

---

164. Lovejoy, *Religious Enthusiasm*, 2–3, 70, 26.

165. Casebolt, "'It Was Not Taught,'" 66–73.

166. Like the other visionaries I have cited, she seems to have been sincere in her conviction that she was the object of direct, divine inspiration. Of course, as third parties, none of us can make empirical observations on the purported communications transacted between the divine mind and the mind of Ellen Harmon.

167. Ellen Harmon's first and closest disciples, including Father Pearson, Joseph Bates, and others such as the J. N. Andrews family, all shared one decisive characteristic. They all evidenced poor judgment in believing that Miller's and Snow's farfetched exposition of the scriptures was commonsense, literal exegesis. It was due to their collective evaluation of Ellen Harmon's gifts that she became *corporately* accepted as a prophetic authority. In 1845 she began to acquire a prophetic authority whose status gave her the authority to inform her disciples of who had the "true light" on unique SDA dogmas. Elsewhere I have documented how Joseph Bates, in particular, was temperamentally inclined to fanciful date setting. See Knight, *Joseph Bates*, 20, 64.

Cry, when she "saw" that God had given Crosier the "true light" regarding a novel Extended Atonement and Investigative Judgment doctrine, she concluded that their allegorical-historicist method of interpreting the Bible was reliable.

Ecclesiastes 4:12 states that a "threefold cord is not quickly broken." In Ellen Harmon's case, the three strands that could not be broken were: 1) her conviction that she was favored by direct divine revelation; 2) her conviction that the numerous biblical verses cited by Miller and Snow really could predict an exact day of the Second Coming; and 3) her conviction that Miller also had received regular angelic and divine guidance in his interpretation of the Apocalypse. She not only promulgated the thesis that Miller's theories were due to his direct, angelic guidance, but also claimed that S. S. Snow's Midnight Cry was divine "light" on her path to heaven and that Crosier had received the "true light" in regard to what happened invisibly in the heavenly sanctuary on the fatidic date of October 22, 1844.

As a consequence, the inextricably intertwined expositions of these men are considered to have been prophetically authenticated by Ellen G. White. As a result, mainstream Seventh-day Adventism does not consider it permissible to subject their expositions to textual and contextual scriptural analysis, or historical falsification. Because Ellen White has stamped their work, and Uriah Smith's, with her prophetic imprimatur, they are considered untouchable—despite solid biblical and historical evidence that their expositions have been falsified by history and textual analysis. Ellen G. White's confirmation has been elevated above scriptural evidence and has become a replacement for actual biblical study.

Meanwhile, all the signs of the end, such as the 1755 Lisbon earthquake, the 1780 Dark Day, the 1833 meteorite shower, and the purported collapse of the Ottoman Empire on August 11, 1840 recede into a distant past. Yet, according to SDA chronology, the "time of the end" still started in 1798—now a quarter of a millennium in the past. Even more incongruous is the assertion that the Midnight Cry happened in 1844. Is it conceivable that the Second Coming should happen at a couple centuries past Midnight? For

Ellen Harmon, the Midnight Cry irrevocably happened in 1844 because Miller had fifteen biblical proofs for this date. From this date onward she repeatedly, *ad infinitum*, predicted, using every biblical simile, metaphor, and symbol, that the Second Coming was only a few months distant. On January 31, 1849, she chastises persons who imagine that time "may continue a few years more," with the clear inference that time would last less than a few years. In 1850, she *quotes* her "accompanying angel" as saying: "Time is almost finished." About the same time, she contrasts persons like herself who have been "years learning" and claims that current converts "will have to learn [the same doctrines] in a few months." She quotes her accompanying angel: "Said the angel, Jesus' work is almost finished in the sanctuary. It is no time to be stupid now; a quick work will the Lord do upon the earth, the four angels will soon let go the four winds."[168]

It is time to admit that for twelve-year-old Ellen Harmon there was the dichotomous, existential choice between a destiny of hell before Millerism and the New Jerusalem and heaven after Millerism. She had the ecstatic, bodily experience of being saved through what her Methodist class leader labelled the "erroneous theory" of Miller. As 1844 became 1845, history demonstrated that Miller's "erroneous theory" contained flawed signs and invalid time intervals. The specious, farfetched nature of at least fourteen of Miller's fifteen mathematical proofs has been tacitly

---

168. For a small sample of extreme imminence rhetoric, see White, *Ellen G. White, Letters and Manuscripts*, 125, 136, 152, 153, 163, 168, 173, 177–78, 183, 205. She uses expressions like Christ's Second Coming is "very, very soon," or "that time can last but a very little longer," or the "sealing time is very short, and soon will be over," in a vague but extremely imminent sense several times. On other occasions she is more specific, saying, for example, that the "time of their [sinners] salvation is passed," or "Jesus is soon to step out from between God and man" and the sealing will then be accomplished, or "time is very short," or "the angels [holding the four winds] are letting go; the sword, famine, and pestilence are coming speedily," "every case is fixed," or the "jewels are almost made up. They are made up but they do not shine. It is the swift messengers that are to do the work," or the "time of trouble, it will come right early." Lastly expressions like: "Closing up, closing up, closing up, closing up. But two things—heaven or hell, life or death, now, now" clearly teach that history is "closing up . . . now, now."

conceded by SDA apologists.[169] The fifteenth proof, based on Dan 8:14 underwent reinterpretation based on the identical, fallacious, allegorical-typological-historicist method that resulted in the failed prediction of October 22, 1844 for the Second Coming.

[169]. See Donald E. Casebolt's forthcoming book, *Father Miller's Daughter: Ellen Harmon White*, for a detailed analysis of fourteen of Miller's failed proofs. These include the failure of the Ottoman Empire to collapse in 1840; Miller's "a prophetic day equals a thousand years principal" as applied to Hosea and Luke; the Seven Times (2520 years) of the Gentiles; the 1335-year prophecy; the 1290-year prophecy; the 1260-year prophecy; the Gog and Magog prophecy; and the potpourri of the sequential chronology of the seven churches and four beasts of Revelation. It also deconstructs S. S. Snow's contorted Midnight Cry explanation, or "tarrying time" justification for Miller's original choice of March 21, 1844 for the Second Coming. It also highlights the significance of the missing shut-door, missing Sabbath halo, missing Messianic High Priest, and his missing golden censor that Ellen Harmon never envisioned in her First Vision. As part of his fifteen chronological proofs that 1843–1844 would be the end of the world, Miller insisted that the "daily sacrifice" of Dan 8 must symbolize pagan Rome ruling from 168 BC to AD 508 (exactly 666 years) and had nothing to do with the Old Testament sacrificial system. Following Miller, Ellen G. White asserted that "sacrifice" was an inaccurately supplied English word by the King James Version's translators. ("I have seen that the 1843 chart was directed by the hand of the Lord, and that it should not be altered.... Then I saw in relation to the 'daily' (Dan 8:12) that the word sacrifice was supplied by man's wisdom and does not belong to the text and that the Lord gave a correct view of it to those who gave the judgment hour cry.") Miller stated that he could find no occurrence of the Hebrew word translated "daily sacrifice" outside of Daniel. Ellen G. White committed an obvious factual error in adopting Miller's analysis. The Hebrew term translated "daily sacrifice" occurs about two dozen times in Num 28 and 29 where Yahweh gives detailed instructions for celebrating the twice "daily sacrifice" routinely, as well as on special Jewish holidays. The significance of this is that the Miller/Ellen Harmon interpretation of "the daily sacrifice" is a critical part of the 1843 chart that Ellen G. White claimed was endorsed by God. Not only this, but she also included it in the remodeled Otis Nichols 1850–1851 chart which was supervised under her personal inspiration. This 1850–1851 chart was the foundation of Ellen G. White's evangelism in the 1850s just like Miller's 1843 chart was the pictorial foundation for the Millerite movement. Demonstrating this obvious factual error in both charts reveals a "testable, falsifiable" hypothesis underlying White's allegorical-typological-historicist schema. Finally, the legendary basis for Ellen G. White's assertion that the Waldenses kept the Sabbath since apostolic times is dissected. Coincidently, the associated interpretation that a supreme papacy massacred the pure church of the Waldenses for 1260 years is also debunked.

Ellen Harmon was never able to separate her subjective experience of being saved through Millerism from the objective mistakes inherent in it. Ironically, Miller himself admitted his error. Ellen Harmon could never admit the error that Miller admitted. The denomination Ellen G. White cofounded has thus far found it impossible to admit that its founder made the same error that Miller confessed to. How could it, if Ellen G. White's visions were direct emanations of the divine Mind? However, more than two centuries after the "time of the end" began purportedly in 1798, and a quarter of a millennium after the 1755 Lisbon earthquake purportedly fulfilled an end-times prophecy, it is time to admit the unavoidable truth. Ellen G. White was mistaken in her evaluation of S. S. Snow's date-setting Midnight Cry. Or, as Robert Olson said, she misinterpreted her First Vision. Continuing to insist that multiple Millerite cosmic signs and "exact" prophetic intervals have any legitimacy, undermines the credibility of all other biblical truths which the SDA church holds dear.

> "We are all tattooed in our cradles with the beliefs of our tribe; the record may seem superficial, but it is indelible."
> Oliver Wendell Holmes

Miller was tattooed by a long tradition of allegorical-typological-historicism. This is demonstrated in my forthcoming book, *Father Miller's Daughter: Ellen Harmon White*. Despite its record of having its Reformation-era predictions falsified, Miller reinterpreted it by discovering new dates and events three centuries later. Ellen Harmon was tattooed by her experience with Miller's millennial enthusiasm from age twelve to sixteen. As Ellen Harmon became Ellen G. White, her two thousand visions resulted in eight thousand letters, five thousand periodical articles and countless speaking engagements. The testimonies emanating from these thousands of communications imprinted an indelible tattoo on scores of SDA thought leaders, on a disciplined ecclesiological organization, on a collection of Millerite era interpretations, and on the corporate consciousness of about twenty million SDA laypersons. It remains to be seen if an exegetical and historical analysis of allegorical-typological-historicism can efface this seemingly ineradicable tattoo.

Bibliography

Arain, M., et al. "Maturation of the Adolescent Brain." *Neuropsychiatry Disease and Treatment* 9 (2013) 449–461.
Baker, Benjamin. "They lived near the bridge where we went over." *Spectrum* 42 (2014) 45–51.
Baker, Delbert W. *The Unknown Prophet: Before Ellen White, God Used William Ellis Foy.* Washington, DC: Review and Herald, 1987.
Burt, Merlin D. "The Day-Dawn of Canandaigua, New York: Reprint of a Significant Millerite Adventist Journal." *Andrews University Seminary Studies* (2006) 317–30.
———. "Elizabeth Haines." In *The Ellen G. White Encyclopedia*, edited by Denis Fortin and Jerry Moon, 393–94. Hagerstown, MD: Review and Herald, 2013.
———. "The Historical Background, Interconnected Development, and Integration of the Doctrines of the Sanctuary, the Sabbath, and Ellen G. White's Role in Sabbatarian Adventism from 1844–1849." PhD diss., Andrews University, 2002.
———. "The 'Shut Door' and Ellen White's Visions." In *The Ellen G. White Letters & Manuscripts with Annotations: 1845–1859*, annotated by Roland Karlman, 41–61. Hagerstown, MD: Review and Herald, 2014.
Casebolt, Donald. "'It Was Not Taught Me by Man': Ellen White's Visions and 2 Esdras." *Spectrum* 46 (2018) 66–73.
Castor, Helen. *Joan of Arc.* New York: Harper, 2015.
Coon, Roger W. *The Great Visions of Ellen G. White.* Hagerstown, MD: Review and Herald, 1992.
Cottrell, Raymond F. "Sanctuary Debate: A Question of Method." *Spectrum* 10 (1980) 16–26.
Crocombe, Jeff. "'A Feast of Reason': The Roots of William Miller's Biblical Interpretation and Its Influence on the Seventh-day Adventist Church." PhD diss., University of Queensland, 2011.
Daily, Steve. *Ellen G. White: A Psychobiography.* Conneaut Lake, PA: Page Publishing, 2020.

Bibliography

Doan, Ruth Alden. *The Miller Heresy, Millennialism, and American Culture.* Philadelphia: Temple University Press, 1987.

"Exposition of Matthew, 24th Chapter." *Signs of the Times,* June 21, 1843, 121–28.

Fortin, Denis and Jerry Moon. "For Jesus and Scripture: The Life of Ellen G. White." In *The Ellen G. White Encyclopedia,* edited by Denis Fortin and Jerry Moon, 18–95. Hagerstown, MD: Review and Herald, 2013.

———. "Visions of Ellen G. White." In *The Ellen G. White Encyclopedia,* edited by Denis, Fortin and Jerry Moon, 1249–53. Hagerstown, MD: Review and Herald, 2013.

Foy, William E. *The Christian Experience of William E. Foy: Together with the Two Visions He Received Jan. and Feb. 1842.* Portland, ME: John and Charles Pearson, 2011.

Froom, Leroy Edwin. *The Prophetic Faith of Our Fathers: PreReformation and Reformation, Restoration, and Second Departure 2.* Washington, DC: Review and Herald, 1948.

———. *The Prophetic Faith of Our Fathers: The Historical Development of Prophetic Interpretation 3.* Washington, DC: Review and Herald, 1946.

Hale, Apollos. *The Second Advent Manual.* Boston: J. V. Himes, 1843.

Harris, Ruth. *Lourdes: Body and Spirit in the Secular Age.* London: Penguin, 1999.

Harrison, Kathryn. *Joan of Arc: A Life Transfigured.* New York: Doubleday, 2014.

Hoyt, Frederick. "Trial of Elder I. Dammon Reported for the Piscataquis Farmer." *Spectrum* 17 (1987) 29–36.

———. "We Lifted Up Our Voices Like a Trumpet: Millerites in Portland, Maine." *Spectrum* 17 (1987) 15–22.

Jacobs, Enoch. "If the Vision Tarry, Wait for It." *The Western Midnight Cry!!!* April 13, 1844, 33–40.

———. "Scriptural Test of Saving Faith." *The Western Midnight Cry!!!* March 23, 1844, 17–24.

Jennisken, Peter. *Meteorite Showers and Their Parent Comets.* Cambridge: Cambridge University Press, 2006.

Jones, Henry. "Fearful Sights, Great Signs." *Signs of the Times,* February 15, 1843, 169–77.

———. "Fearful Sights, Great Signs, &c." *The Midnight Cry,* November 22, 1842, 177–85.

Knight, George. *Joseph Bates: The Real Founder of Seventh-day Adventism.* Hagerstown, MD: Review and Herald, 2004.

Knight, George R. *Millennial Fever and the End of the World.* Boise, ID: Pacific, 1993.

———. *Walking with Ellen White.* Hagerstown, MD: Review and Herald, 1999.

Levterov, Theodore N. *The Development of the Seventh-day Adventist Understanding of Ellen G. White's Prophetic Gift.* New York: Peter Lang, 2015.

Bibliography

Lovejoy, David S. *Religious Enthusiasm in the New World: Heresy to Revolution.* Cambridge, MA: Harvard University Press, 1985.

Marini, Stephen A. *Radical Sects of Revolutionary New England.* Cambridge, MA: Harvard University Press, 1982.

Miller, William. *Evidence from Scripture and History of the Second Coming of Christ.* Boston: Himes, 1842.

———. *Evidences from Scripture and History of the Second Coming of Christ About the Year A.D. 1843.* 3rd edition. Syracuse, NY: T.A. and S.F. Smith, 1835.

———. *Evidences from Scripture and History of the Second Coming of Christ About the Year A.D. 1843 and of His personal reign of 1000 years.* Vermont: Vermont Telegraph Office, 1833.

———. "A Lecture on the Signs of the Present Times." *Signs of the Times*, March 20, 1840, 1–8.

Misson, Maximillien. *A Cry from the Desert: Or Testimonials of the Miraculous Things Lately Come to Pass in the Cevennes, Verified upon Oath, and by Other Proofs.* London: Paternoster-Row, 1707.

Nichol, Francis D. *The Midnight Cry.* Washington, DC: Review and Herald, 1944.

Olson, Robert W., and Roger W. Coon. "Ellen G. White: A Chronology." In *The Ellen G. White Encyclopedia*, edited by Denis Fortin and Jerry Moon, 112–14. Hagerstown, MD: Review and Herald, 2013.

Peterson, Donald I. "Visions or Seizures." Boise, ID: Pacific, 1988.

Poirier, Tim. "Black Forerunner to Ellen White: William E. Foy." *Spectrum* 17 (1987) 23–28.

Rowe, David L. *God's Strange Work: William Miller and the End of the World.* Grand Rapids: Eerdmans, 2008.

Smith, Uriah. *Daniel and Revelation: Response of History to the Voice of Prophecy.* Battle Creek, MI: Review and Herald, 1897.

———. *Daniel and the Revelation.* Nashville: Southern, 1944.

Snow, S. S. "Letter from S. S. Snow." *The Midnight Cry*, February 22, 1844.

———. "Letter from S. S. Snow." *The Midnight Cry*, June 27, 1844.

———. "Behold, The Bridegroom Cometh; Go Ye Out to Meet Him." *The True Midnight Cry*, August 22, 1844.

Storrs, George. "Go Ye Out to Meet Him. The Tenth Day of the Seventh Month." *The Advent Herald, and Signs of the Times Reporter*, October 16, 1844.

Strayer, Brian E. *J. N. Loughborough: The Last of the Adventist Pioneers.* Hagerstown, MD: Review and Herald, 2014.

Valentine, Gilbert. *J. N. Andrews: Mission Pioneer, Evangelist, and Thought Leader.* Nampa, ID: Pacific, 2020.

Walters, Kathie. *Child Prophets of the Huguenots.* Translated by Claire Uyttebrouck. Macon, GA: Good News Fellowship Ministries, 2016.

White, Arthur. *Ellen G. White: The Early Years, 1827–1862*, vol. 1. Washington, DC: Review and Herald, 1985.

Bibliography

White, Ellen G. *Christian Experience and Teaching of Ellen G. White.* Mountain View, CA: Pacific, 1940.

———. "Communications: Dear Young Friends," *The Youth's Instructor,* December 1852, 20–22.

———. *Ellen G. White: Letters & Manuscripts With Annotations, 1845–1859.* Hagerstown, MD: Review and Herald, 2014.

———. *The Great Controversy.* Oakland, CA: Pacific, 1888.

———. *The Great Controversy.* Mountain View, CA: Review and Herald, 1911.

———. *The Great Controversy.* Mountain View, CA: Pacific, 1950.

———. *Life Sketches.* Mountain View, CA: Pacific, 1915.

———. *Selected Messages.* vol. 1. Washington, DC: Review and Herald, 1958.

———. *Spiritual Gifts.* vol. 2. Washington, DC: Review and Herald, 1945.

———. *Spiritual Gifts.* vol. 1. Battle Creek, MI: Review & Herald, 1858.

White, James S. "A Word to the '"Little Flock.'" Brunswick, ME: James White, 1847.

White, James, and Ellen G. White. *Life Sketches: Ancestry, Early Life, Christian Experience and Extensive Labors of Elder James White, and his Wife Mrs. Ellen G. White.* Battle Creek, MI: Steam Press, 1880.

Wigger, John H. *Taking Heaven by Storm: Methodism and the Rise of Popular Christianity in America.* Urbana, IL: University of Illinois Press, 2001.

Winship, Michael P. *Making Heretics.* Princeton: Princeton University Press, 2002.